J. M. Clark

C. ADDISON HICKMAN

J. M. Clark

Columbia Essays on the Great Economists
Donald J. Dewey, General Editor

◆▶◀▶◀▶

J. M. CLARK

◆▶◀▶◀▶

C. Addison Hickman

COLUMBIA UNIVERSITY ♛ NEW YORK AND LONDON
PRESS   1975

Library of Congress Cataloging in Publication Data

Hickman, Charles Addison, 1916–
   J. M. Clark
   (Columbia essays on the great economists)
   Bibliography: p.
1. Clark, John Maurice, 1884–
        HB119.C53H52   330'.092'4   75–5649
          ISBN 0–231–03187–4
          ISBN 0–231–03918–2 pbk.

A Note on the Citation of Source

If only a casual allusion, a quotation of a few words, or a phrase so familiar as to be in the public domain is involved, no more than sparse identification will be given. Where a quotation or allusion of some significance is involved, from writings referring primarily to Clark but not by him, there will be sufficient identification to cue into the bibliography. Where the material is neither by Clark nor primarily about him, enough identification will be provided to locate the source if the reader so desires. If, however, the source is in Clark's work, and is of substantial character, symbols as given below will be used. All of these cue into the bibliography. Whenever possible, for the sake of simplicity and the convenience of the reader, anthologies are cited rather than the original journal articles.

Symbols used to identify citations from Clark:

AS: *Alternative to Serfdom* (1st ed.)
CDP: *Competition as a Dynamic Process*
EI: *Economic Institutions and Human Welfare*
ESS: *Encyclopaedia of the Social Sciences*, "Overhead Costs"
EM: "The Empire of Machines"
GC: "Government Control of Industry"
ME: "Mathematical Economists and Others"
OC: *Studies in the Economics of Overhead Costs*
PSE: *Preface to Social Economics*
SC: *Social Control of Business* (1st ed.)
SCC: "Some Current Cleavages Among Economists"
SF: *Strategic Factors in Business Cycles*
UN: United Nations Report
WC: "Toward a Concept of Workable Competition"

Acknowledgments

A number of publishers, journals, and individuals have given permission to quote. This courtesy is greatly appreciated. The grantors of permission include:

The Academy of Political Science, publishers of *Political Science Quarterly*, passages from three reviews by J. M. Clark (Hicks, Cassel, and Hayek), as cited in *Sources* (for *J. M. Clark and his Peers*), p. 83.

The American Economic Association, publishers of *American Economic Review*, passages from a review by J. M. Clark (Pigou) and an obituary-biographical sketch (Veblen), also by J. M. Clark, both as cited in *Sources* (for *J. M. Clark and his Peers*), p. 83. Also passages from an article by J. M. Clark, "Economic Means— To What Ends?" cited in the text as EI 14, 31–33 and also included in the Bibliography. Also a review by Kenneth E.

Boulding (Clark's *Economic Institutions and Human Welfare*), which is included in the Bibliography.

Dr. M. J. Aronson, editor and copyright holder, *Journal of Social Philosophy*, passages from an obituary-biographical sketch by J. M. Clark (Hobson), as cited in *Sources* (for *J. M. Clark and his Peers*), p. 84.

The Trustees of Columbia University in the City of New York, passages from a chapter by J. M. Clark in *National Policy for Economic Welfare at Home and Abroad*, ed. by Robert Lekachman, cited in the text as EI 116, 168–69 and also included in the Bibliography.

Harper and Row, Publishers, Inc., passages from a chapter by J. M. Clark in *Goals of Economic Life*, ed. by Dudley Ward, cited in the text as EI 59, 66 and also included in the Bibliography.

Holt, Rinehart and Winston, Inc., passages from *Preface to Social Economics*, by J. M. Clark, which is included in the Bibliography.

Alfred A. Knopf, Inc., passages from *Economic Institutions and Human Welfare*, p. 207, by J. M. Clark, copyright © 1957, and from *Alternative to Serfdom*, by J. M. Clark, copyright © 1948, both of which are included in the Bibliography.

Macmillan Publishing Co., Inc., passages from entry by J. M. Clark (John Bates Clark), in *International Encyclopedia of the Social Sciences*, ed. David L. Sills, Vol. 2, pp. 504–8, copyright © 1968, cited in *Sources* (for *J. M. Clark and his Peers*), p. 84.

W. W. Norton and Co., Inc., passages from *Economics in the Twentieth Century*, by Theo Suranyi-Unger, ed. by Edwin R. A. Seligman, translated by Noel D. Moulton, copyright © 1931, 1959, which is included in the Bibliography.

The Quarterly Journal of Economics, passages from a review by J. M. Clark (Sombart), as cited in *Sources* (for *J. M. Clark and his Peers*), p. 83.

Henry W. Spiegel, copyright holder, passages from a chapter by J. M. Clark (on J. B. Clark), in *The Development of Economic Thought*, ed. by Henry W. Spiegel, which is cited in *Sources* (for *J. M. Clark and his Peers*), p. 84. Professor Spiegel is especially to be thanked for the graciousness of his response.

The University of Chicago Press, passages from *Studies in the*

Economics of Overhead Costs, by J. M. Clark, copyright © 1923; *Social Control of Business*, 1st ed., by J. M. Clark, copyright © 1926; chapter by J. M. Clark in *Methods in Social Science*, ed. by Stuart A. Rice, copyright © 1931, and cited in *Sources* (for *J. M. Clark and his Peers*), p. 84. All three are included in the Bibliography. Also passages from two book reviews by J. M. Clark (Marshall and Cooley), in *Journal of Political Economy*, as cited in *Sources* (for *J. M. Clark and his Peers*), p. 83, 84.

The Yale Review, passages from an article by J. M. Clark, "The Empire of Machines," which is included in the Bibliography.

Edward H. Witkowski played an invaluable role in helping assemble the lifetime writings of J. M. Clark, as well as assisting in the preparation of a massive bibliography on Clark, both of which have been vital to the distillation process represented by this essay. Anthony V. Catanese, Sally Jo Wright, Parvez Mahmud, and Shridhar Shrimali have given effective help in the mechanics of manuscript preparation and proofing. More subtle debts are owed to my departmental colleagues, who have excused much because of my known preoccupation with this essay, and to my wife, Dorothy, who has allowed another member—an eminent long-time professor of economics at Columbia University—to enter our family during the past several years.

Contents

Contents

J. M. Clark

Introduction

An essay purporting to bear the title "J. M. Clark" is both presumptuous and an exercise in frustration for the author, if not for the reader. Clark published his first book in 1910, his last in 1961; and books, journal articles, essays, or professional writing of some sort appeared in every year from 1910 to 1963. The sheer volume of Clark's work is matched by its wide-ranging character, as Clark wrote at a demanding professional level in at least a dozen fields of economics as well as on the edge of economics. Furthermore, it soon becomes apparent that, to Clark, almost everything he did was interconnected with his other work —thus necessitating a search for the pervasive ideas, the continuing threads, that provide this interconnection.

Further, although Clark is lucid, incisive, and on occasion eloquent, he is also very hard going in spots. He is so meticulous, so exact, so detailed, and sometimes so complex in his determined avoidance of mathematics and his insistence on prose, that one stifles an occasional base craving for an equation or for a simplistic or even a simple page. As J. K. Galbraith commented in his review (see Bibliography) of a major 1957 anthology of Clark's work: "Mr. Clark is not to be read for relaxation. His carefully qualified and carefully thought-out sentences have to be taken slowly. I have a friend who argues that this is the way a scholar ought to write. If it is all too easy the reading will be at a greater pace than the mind can handle. I am a little suspicious of this argument. It could justify some terrible prose. But I am willing to allow it in the present case. Mr. Clark takes time and is always worth it" (p. 3).

Certain inescapable decisions had to be made at the outset in order to undertake this venture at all. First, the book is limited to the published work of J. M. Clark and, as the Bibliographic Note makes clear, not even to all of that. No attempt is made to cope with the vast array of letters, memos, and other materials by or to Clark that would go into the making of a treatise or a definitive intellectual biography. The collection of John Maurice Clark Papers (1920–63) held by the Columbia University Library includes some 25,000 items.

Neither, alas, is it possible here to fully trace or detail the large part of Clark's professional career that did not involve publication. He was a faculty member at Colorado College, Amherst, the University of Chicago, and (from 1926 through 1958, and after that as a professionally active Professor Emeritus) at Columbia University. As a teacher, he reached directly or indirectly large numbers of students, directed a host of doctoral dissertations, and strongly influenced his colleagues on a face-to-face basis as well as through his publications.

Also virtually excluded, except as it may be reflected in the Bibliography, was his active professional service as a consultant or as a member (and often chairman) of commissions, task forces, and committees, both private and governmental, dealing with a wide range of pressing matters—economic and otherwise. Among these associations were the National Resources Planning Board, the Twentieth Century Fund, the Committee on Freedom of the Press, the National Recovery Administration, the Office of Price

Administration, and the Attorney General's National Committee to Study the Anti-Trust Laws. He also often appeared as an expert witness before Congressional committees and like bodies. When Columbia University granted him an honorary degree in 1954, the citation noted that he was "always freely at the government's disposal and aided well his country." As the 1952 recipient of the Francis A. Walker medal given by the American Economic Association (at long intervals), he was obviously more than merely the grist for a bibliography. Yet, if this essay is to have manageable focus, his published work must serve as inadequate but necessary proxy for the man.

Another limitation on the ambitions of this essay must also be imposed. Although it is tempting and might be insightful to trace the changes in Clark's work over a half century, and even to relate them to the changing conditions under which he wrote, this would be a project too vast to fit into a book of modest size. Further, the remarkable thing about Clark's work is how little the main thrust changed, not how much. His immediate focus did change, his tone grew milder and gentler, and he sought always to update his work, but his central ideas and his basic approach were set early and proved remarkably durable.

There is also an additional temptation, and a beguiling one, that must be resisted if the focus of this essay is to be upon J. M. Clark and his work, taken at its face and not upon its genesis. The relationship between J. M. Clark and his equally celebrated father, a leading neoclassicist with, however, some prophetic insights into the limitations of the market and a powerful ethical bent, would be of interest to any intellectual historian and it is a human-interest story in the bargain. That this relationship was close, and that J. M. Clark's debt to his father was great, is attested to by his frequent acknowledgments of that debt as well as by his occasional elaborate efforts to rationalize an evident divergence from his father's views. He wrote his Ph.D. thesis under his father's direction; he co-authored with his father a revision of *The Control of Trusts*, he dedicated *Studies in the Economics of Overhead Costs* to his father, "who started me in this field of inquiry"; and in the preface to his last book, *Competition as a Dynamic Process*, he traces his interest in dynamics to his father's belief that dynamics are the fulfillment of statics. J. M. Clark's own appraisal of J. B. Clark's work is found, in small part, in the "Peers" section at the close of this essay. Meanwhile, even this intriguing line of inquiry must be put aside.

A final decision (made at the outset) is to decline to attempt an encyclopedic coverage of all that he wrote, or even of all the major fields in which he did significant work and achieved stature. In addition to the matters to be stressed here, Clark did serious and respected work in such divergent fields as railway and public utility rates, basing-point pricing, the theory of regulated enterprise, long-range planning, the history of economic thought (with a brief excursion into the sociology of knowledge), the economics of war and of postwar conversion, the economics of public works, the NRA, and wage-price theory and policy. Sadly, although failure to consider these bodies of work tends to diminish and oversimplify his sprawling scholarly universe, space constraints so dictate. Perhaps the partial Bibliography appended to this essay may restore some sense of sweep and range—or it may only reinforce the sense of diminution.

Even with the decision to narrow the focus to four fields—microeconomics (largely overhead costs and workable competition), macroeconomics (mostly Clark's "strategic factors" approach, the acceleration principle, and his policy prescriptions), the economics of welfare (stressing social control, the meaning of welfare, and voluntary pluralism), and an examination of the discipline of economics (especially its scope, methods, and premises)—it is apparent that a lot of territory is yet to be covered.

Where should the emphasis be? Although an attempt has been made to cover all four of these sectors at some minimal level of adequacy, some parts of Clark's major work deserve compensatory highlighting. His contributions on overhead costs, workable competition, the acceleration principle, and social control constitute his remaining claim on conventional reading lists. Yet, his pioneering and prophetic work in the field of welfare, and his sane and healing advice to his economist colleagues concerning their discipline, may be of at least equal import. Hence, if there is any disproportion between the space allocation within this essay and the familiar contributions with which Clark is readily linked, it is in the interests of restoring the whole man—a man who more than most men must be seen whole.

This compensatory redress of balance does pose an obvious danger. Bertrand Russell remarked long ago that all animals who have been carefully observed turn out to display the national characteristics of their observers: animals studied by Americans rush about frantically and finally achieve the desired result by chance; animals observed by Germans sit still and think and finally evolve the answer out of their inner consciousness. Let Clark not suffer a similar fate at my hands!

Now to Clark's single most persistent theoretical interest—microeconomics.

◄ 1 ►

Microeconomics

Clark's contributions to microeconomics, especially price theory, were legion. He wrote in this field, at a rigorous technical level, for most of his long career. He worked in the vanguard of the profession in such fields as railway and public utility rate theory and policy, basing-point pricing and other spatial price theory, wage-price relationships, the relation between prices and full employment, cost-push inflation, and price and wage control during and after wars. This is but a partial gleaning from a continuing outpouring of articles, essays, and books written between 1910 and 1963. Most of this work, almost from the start of his career, had influence upon the economics of his era. Some of his work in the fields enumerated above remain as early building blocks in now-elaborate structures of economic analysis. They also remain as models of precise, meticulous, and dispassionate study, done by a man who was a theorist with a craving for relevant data.

Out of all the vast assemblage of writing in the micro field which can be attributed to Clark, his work in two areas—the study of overhead costs and the development of a concept of workable (or effective) competition—has somehow become a major part of his known legacy to our generation of economists. In both cases, the core ideas appear in embryonic form in his 1910 doctoral dissertation, and they persist in his 1961 valedictory book as major themes.

THE STUDY OF OVERHEAD COSTS

His classic work in this field, *Studies in the Economics of Overhead Costs*, appeared in 1923. Much of what follows is derived from that source, although Clark wrote about this question long before and after 1923.

The term "overhead costs" is defined by Clark as a related group of ideas having a common element: the fact that these costs cannot be traced or allocated to particular units of product, divisions of the business, or classes of customers. The basic fact underlying this concept of overhead costs, Clark emphasized time and again, is the economy—and the problems—that come with increased utilization of productive equipment that has idle capacity.

The differential costs have to be covered by any unit of sales if that unit is worth taking as a separate increment. The overhead costs have to be at least roughly covered by the business as an entity in the long run, but in the short run they need not be covered. The portion of these overhead costs borne by any given sector of the business, or any product, is a matter of business policy and not of necessity dictated by costs. Sensitivity of demand is likely to be a primary consideration in this decision.

Overhead costs are important, of course, because modern industrialism dictates machine technology and heavy applications of capital. Clark demonstrates that, to some extent, overhead costs are significant throughout all sectors of the economy—small business, agriculture, consumption, government, and labor. Nevertheless, the most obvious cases in point have been found in capital-intensive industry. It is no accident that one of Clark's major preoccupations during the first decade of his career was with railroad and public utility rates and costs.

The machine, Clark reminds us, craves full utilization:

> This mechanical slave has absolutely none of labor's thirst for variety. Uniformity is his passion; continuous operation his religion. He is tireless: his capacity limited only by the hours of the day. And if any of it is not used it is lost: he cannot fill his idle time with side-occupations. Viewed as an animal he is one whose instinctive inheritance prescribes every act of his life. Minor changes in patterns of behavior require a surgical operation; major ones require that he be born again. Hence he yearns to specialize and to turn out indefinitely large quantities of his specialty. (OC, p. 9)

The preponderance and pervasiveness of overhead costs in the economy have at least four principal effects, as envisaged by Clark. These include (1) the widespread and necessary resort to price discrimination; (2) the tendency for monopoly power to be somewhat extended; (3) the aggravating effect upon the business cycle; and (4) the highlighting of the fact that although the support of the labor force is a true overhead cost of industry and society, the burden of idle capacity and resultant unemployment is often borne by the worker.

Discrimination. Clark claims that

> If one had to choose a motto of six words, expressing the most central economic consequence of overhead cost, the first choice might fall upon some such phrase as: "Full utilization is worth its cost," but a close second would be: "Discrimination is the secret of efficiency." This last, to be sure, needs to be taken with a proviso: one must know where to stop. (OC, p. 416)

The economic grounds for discrimination are obvious. A business may or may not be covering all overhead costs, but in either instance added business will not add to the overhead (if at less than capacity). Thus, such sales will incur gain at anything above differential cost. This is subject to one major proviso: the new business must be kept separate from existing business, in order that existing earnings not be jeopardized. Thus, each part of the business must cover differential cost and as much of the common overhead as it can. How much it can pay toward overhead will depend upon the sensitivity of demand to reduced price, the feasibility of confining the lower price to new business, and the possibility that other firms might be goaded into reprisals.

Whether or not discrimination is in the social interest depends largely upon whether the added business is a net social addition or merely a diversion of demand from one producer to another. Clark concludes:

If the new business represents a true addition to the social dividend, the interest of the concern making the discrimination corresponds with that of society. If the new business is merely taken from competitors (or shifted from the consumption of different goods) whose costs of production behave in the same way, then there is no social gain, but merely a loss to the competitors which corresponds to the private gain made by the business originating the discrimination. In such a case, the result is likely to be reprisals which may turn the gain of the original business into a loss or bring on a general state of cut-throat competition. On the other hand, if fear of reprisals prevents all discrimination, chances may be lost for developing socially worth while business. (ESS, 11:512)

Combination and monopoly power.   Where single plants are large, the tendency toward both vertical and horizontal combination is strong. Because large plants usually accompany the use of large proportions of fixed capital, such capital-intensive technology seems to be conducive to combination and the possible range of monopoly control. It is also the industries of large overhead costs which frequently spawn the cutthroat competition that may also lead either to combination or collusion. Large overhead costs also constitute an obstacle to the free entry of new firms, limit their number, and increase their risks. All of this would seem to make the force of "potential competition," usually a deterrent to the exercise of full monopoly power, somewhat less effective. Yet, Clark believed (long before he fully developed the concept of "workable competition") that the full force of overhead costs and the resultant extension of monopoly power might actually be somewhat blunted. He wrote:

A certain amount of informal common action is inevitable and necessary in modern industry, thus producing a condition which is neither old-fashioned competition nor complete monopoly. Even without definite agreements, the moral and prudential restraints on cut-throat competition are varied and fairly effective. They are in turn limited by potential competition, which also takes many forms and is a loose but fairly adequate form of control. The result is sometimes to reduce efficiency by dividing up the existing business among too many producers, but this itself has its limits, and if the protective controls which industry already possesses are intelligently directed, they may accomplish whatever stimulation of demand is desirable in dull times without reducing the average yield, through the whole business cycle, to less than the living rate which private industry requires. Cut-throat competition is an evil, and the adaptive reactions of industry give rise to further evils in the way of extortion and bulwarked inefficiency. But these evils have natural limits which prevent them from growing to intolerable dimensions. (OC, p. 450)

The aggravating of the business cycle.   As will be noted later in this essay, Clark's contribution to business cycle theory and macroeconomics lies largely in his concept of the acceleration principle. This concept stems directly from the disproportionate growth rates of consumption and capital goods production. Obviously, where capital goods loom large, as they long have in our economy, this principle is of special importance. Thus, although overhead costs may be found throughout the economy, their preponderance in capital-intensive industry links them to the problem of the business cycle.

This is a paradox, according to Clark. Overhead costs make regular and continuous operation especially necessary and profitable, and business loses whenever there is idle capacity. Yet, this very fact of large fixed capacity often leads business to bring these calamities upon itself. The largest businesses, with the greatest overhead costs, are the ones that fluctuate most, especially in regard to employment.

Labor as an overhead cost.   One of the truly innovative insights in

Clark's study of overhead costs was his conception of the support and maintenance of labor as an overhead cost. This led Clark to propose regularized industrial employment and a form of guaranteed annual wage; a variation of this concept in our own era furnishes part of the rationale for the guaranteed annual income.

Clark points out what is obvious *ex post* but was not so apparent *ex ante:* that the cost of maintaining the laborer's health and working capacity is just as inescapably an overhead cost as if machinery were involved. This is true whether the worker is currently employed or not. The only reason this characteristic of the labor force has been hidden to view is the institutional nature of the wage contract, which has historically left the wage earner to care for his own overhead.

The only question is the best distribution of this burden—the best form of social cost-accounting. Clark obviously envisaged a shift of the burden to industry. It has remained for subsequent decades to bring a demand that this particular overhead cost may more properly belong to the larger society, and that government may have a legitimate role to play. This demand has been partly met, of course, through such devices as Social Security and attempts to maintain full employment.

Impact of Clark's overhead costs. Clark believed when he wrote *Studies in the Economics of Overhead Costs* that development of this field of study would give a major thrust toward development of a dynamic economics. He even raises the question whether the study of overhead costs can best function as an "autonomous department of economics" or whether the whole body of economic thought must become an "economics of overhead costs." In point of fact, it has not become either of these. Yet, the concept has had very substantial impact and is found, explicitly, in much of the subsequent literature of economics.

Morris A. Copeland, in a perceptive review (see Bibliography) of this book, saw clearly that its implications for classical theory are disruptive, and that Clark was in genuine logical revolt. Yet, Copeland rather sadly observed, the style is difficult, and being impressed with the complexity of the subject, the author tends to compound that complexity. Thus, Copeland feared that the defense mechanisms of the orthodox economist would enable him to read the book with equanimity, and to conclude (as he noted that a reviewer for one of the standard economic journals had already done) that the book succeeds in correcting certain minor inaccuracies of doctrine. Yet, to Ben B. Seligman, some decades later, this study was Clark's most significant contribution and one of the most incisive studies on the subject ever written—and still relevant and viable.

WORKABLE COMPETITION

Clark's other familiar claim to lasting repute in microeconomics was in his development of the concept of "workable" (or, as he later came to prefer, "effective") competition. The key journal article expounding this idea appeared in 1940; the elaborating, updating, systematizing treatise was published in 1961.

The root idea was not, of course, original with J. M. Clark. For example, his father, the distinguished neoclassicist J. B. Clark, had articulated one of the major elements in the concept of workable competition. In 1907, in the midst of a trust-busting era, J. B. Clark observed that a business may have the form and size of a monopoly, but not its genuine power. Its price may be barely above the cost of production—because a higher price would invite competition. In his *Essentials of Economic Theory*, he concludes:

This is a monopoly in form but not in fact, for it is shorn of its injurious power; and the thing that holds it firmly in check is *potential competition*. The fact that a rival *can* appear and *will* appear if the price goes above the reasonable level at which it stands, induces the corporation to produce goods enough to keep the price at that level. Under such a nearly ideal condition the public would get the full benefit of the economy which very large production gives, notwithstanding that no actual competition would go on. (pp. 380–81)

In *The Control of Trusts*, revised and jointly authored by the Clarks in 1912, the anticipatory term "constructive competition" appears, as does maintaining "tolerant and healthy competition" as a desirable goal of public policy. From these beginnings, amplified in the intervening period in several journal articles, ultimately came the full, formal statement of the concept of workable competition for which J. M. Clark is now widely remembered. This statement came in 1940—to be restated 21 years later in treatise form.

In his famous 1940 journal article, "Toward a Concept of Workable Competition," (see Bibliography) Clark probably created more impact in 15 pages than he did in his 1961 full-length study. Yet, in 1940, just following the decade of Chamberlin and Joan Robinson, the time was ripe and his article proved to be provocative, influential, and controversial.

The primary emphasis in the 1940 paper is upon long-run considerations. He states at the outset:

> At the risk of being convicted of an optimistic bias, I should like to point to certain ways in which long-run forces serve to mitigate the seriousness of the effects of imperfect competition. These considerations center largely in the proposition that long-run curves, both of cost and of demand, are much flatter than short-run curves, and much flatter than the curves which are commonly used in the diagrams of theorists. In fact, it may appear that much of the apparent seriousness of Professor Chamberlin's results derives from what I believe to be the exaggerated steepness of the curves he used to illustrate them. This, of course, is a matter of degree only; but in the field of imperfect competition, and especially in the search for workable adjustments, these matters of degree are of the essence of the problem. (WC, p. 246)

What are the expositors of imperfect competition overlooking or minimizing? Clark believes that even though Edwin H. Chamberlin takes some account of potential competition and substitutions, he markedly underestimates the importance of both. Chamberlin posits potential competition, but he endows the businessman with so little foresight that he carries his output and price policies to the point of inducing potential competition to become actual. Clark argued that some degree of foresight on the part of businessmen would lead them to practice more moderate price and output policy, precisely in order to prevent or discourage potential competition from becoming actual. As for substitution, Clark feels that its range and flexibility has been so vastly expanded by modern industrial technology that it should be weighted very heavily indeed.

Clark set forth, in his 1940 article, a detailed classification of markets, which recognized many factors in addition to the number of sellers and the degree of product differentiation. Joe S. Bain, in his "Price and Production Policies," *A Survey of Contemporary Economics* (AEA), Vol. 1, has created a highly condensed abbreviation of this classification that will suffice for our purposes:

"I.   Pure competition—standard product, known (quoted or supply-governed) price, many sellers at any local market, free entry.
   A.   Perfect competition (perfect factor mobility).
   B.   Imperfect competition (imperfect factor mobility).
      1.   Excess capacity (price less than average cost on average over time).
      2.   No excess capacity.

II.   Modified, intermediate, or hybrid competition.
   A.   Standard products, few sellers, free entry but exit with loss.
      1.   Quoted price, without significant spatial separation of producers.
         a.   Open price.
         b.   Imperfectly known price, chaotic discrimination.
         c.   Open price with limited or occasional departures.
      2.   Supply-governed price (open market).
      3.   Quoted prices, with significant spatial separation of producers.
   B.   Unstandardized products, either many or few sellers.
      1.   Quoted prices.
      2.   Supply-governed prices." (pp. 159–60)

Charles Ferguson, in *A Macroeconomic Theory of Workable Competition*, summarizes the essence of Clark's 1940 (and subsequent) position as a belief that the following conditions will suffice to frequently stimulate a workable competition in real-world markets: "(a) in cases of small numbers, sufficient product heterogeneity to cause uncertainty about competitors' reactions;

(b) a demand curve steep enough to enable the entrepreneur to cover average cost; and (c) an active threat of potential competition and the possibility of intercommodity substitution" (p. 28).

In *Competition as a Dynamic Process*, published in 1961, the paper of 1940 becomes a wide-ranging study, taking into account theoretical and empirical developments of the intervening two decades, and incorporating and synthesizing many of Clark's ideas developed during a professional lifetime. In the process, the sharpness, bite, and timeliness of some of the constituent concepts, such as workable competition, may be muted a bit. The actual exposition, however, is full and lucid. In the Author's Preface, Clark highlights his retrospective view toward the concept and how it seemed to fit as of 1961:

> The present volume is an elaboration of a line of inquiry dating from the author's article entitled "Toward a Concept of Workable Competition," in the June 1940 number of the *American Economic Review*. This article was an attempt to find an escape from the negative conclusions stemming from the Chamberlin-Robinson group of theories, in which it appeared that all feasible forms of competition in industry and trade are defective in the same direction in which monopoly is defective, from the standpoint of the services competition is supposed to render. In the present study, I am shifting the emphasis from "workable" to "effective competition"—a term I think I borrowed from Blackwell Smith—because "workable" stresses mere feasibility and is consistent with the verdict that feasible forms of competition, while tolerable, are still inferior substitutes for that "pure and perfect" competition which has been so widely accepted as a normative ideal. And I have become increasingly impressed that the kind of competition we have, with all its defects—and these are serious—is better than the "pure and perfect" norm, because it makes for progress. Some departures from "pure and perfect" competition are not only inseparable from progress, but necessary to it. The theory of effective competition is dynamic theory. (CDP, p. ix)

Impact of Clark's workable competition. A considerable literature on the subject of workable competition has developed since 1940, partially in response to his incisive paper of that year. The concept in general, and his version in particular, has led to a whole new dialogue in this sphere of economics. Now, three decades or more later, it is apparent that its greatest usefulness was as an antidote and checkpoint for formal simplistic models, whether of perfect or imperfect competition. As a total replacement for these models, and as an adequate basis for public policy, workable competition has been found wanting.

Bain, after condensing Clark's classification of markets, takes issue with its usefulness:

> The state of current knowledge is reflected in the fact that although this classification may contain very pertinent suggestions, we cannot say with certainty whether or not Clark has hit upon the most essential characteristics distinguishing among markets within the oliogopoly category or among markets generally. The writer would object strongly to lumping all differentiated-product industries in one category, regardless of number of sellers, and to neglecting the number of buyers, the durability of output, the difference between relatively easy and very difficult entry in oligopoly, and the time-trend of industry demand. And the extended distinctions among quoted and "supply-governed" prices in oligopoly seem to receive more emphasis than these actually tenuous distinctions may deserve. With Clark we would have automobiles, rubber tires, cigarettes, light bulbs, ladies' dresses, radio sets, optical goods, agricultural equipment, and electrical machinery nested incompatibly together in category II–B–1, although there are significant ascertainable and clearly explicable differences in competitive behavior and price results among these industries. (p. 160)

George Stigler notes in his piece on "Competition" in the *International Encyclopedia of the Social Sciences* that the serious ambiguity of the concept has not yet been diminished. He concludes that how competitive an industry should be in order to be workably competitive is not yet clear, and that even the performance criteria that should be given greatest weight in an application of the concept have not been agreed upon. If two scholars studying a given industry disagree as to its workable competitiveness, Stigler argues, there are no analytical grounds upon which the dispute can be resolved.

Ferguson concurs: "While few economists would now suggest that perfect competition is a suitable norm for public policy, it at least has the advantage of offering an unambiguous policy prescription. Conversely, while workable competition is widely accepted as the appropriate policy norm, there is no widely recognized definition of workability. Agreement upon policy proposals is therefore impossible" (p. 25).

Donald Dewey, in his strongly favorable review (see Bibliography) of *Competition as a Dynamic Process*, nevertheless concludes that:

If this book has a major fault, it lies in an intellectual myopia produced by a lifetime of specialization. Clark probably knows the mechanics of the American economy as well as any man alive, and he is certainly not blind to its minor imperfections. Yet a Socialist could not unfairly contend that Clark's descriptive analysis contains much that is merely rationalization for the status quo. He is prepared to overhaul and rebuild parts of the mechanism; its essential efficiency is taken for granted. In fact, throughout this book, Clark is more concerned to defend existing institutions and policies against libertarian critics of the Simons-Stigler school than to answer the more fundamental indictments of the Socialists. (p. 88)

Yet, the concept of imperfect competition as developed at his hands, largely in 1940, has earned Clark a historic position in the development of an entire subliterature of economics. Ferguson notes that historians of revolution often divide the revolutionary process into five stages: (a) the preparatory period; (b) the revolutionary overthrow of the existing system; (c) the subsequent struggle for power among different factions; (d) the period of excess, and (e) the period of Thermidor, or relaxation of excess. Ferguson concludes that the "empty economic box" controversy and the appearance of Sraffa's paper mark the preparatory period. The almost total acceptance of perfect competition as norm disappeared during the revolutionary era, presumably in the 1930s. The third period, or struggle for power among different factions or ideologies, he finds to be ushered in by Clark's 1940 paper and featured by the myriad definitions of workable competition that followed. Clark's paper thus becomes a benchmark for the termination of one era in the literature and the beginning of another.

There seems to be a contradiction between Clark's rather relaxed position regarding the degree of competition in the market, as reflected in his concept of workable competition, and his strictures (as noted later in this essay) about the limitations of the market and the necessity for social control. There indeed may be a measure of genuine contradiction here. In large part, however, the apparent conflict may be resolved by a parody on the Biblical injunction: "Render unto the market what belongs to the market, and do not intervene all the time, but render unto social control, perhaps voluntary pluralism but also the government, what does not belong to the market."

◂ 2 ▸

Macroeconomics

Clark's preoccupation with dynamics, as well as his concern with welfare, inevitably led him into the business cycle, the full employment problem, and stabilization and full employment policy. Much of his work in these areas, not surprisingly, was concentrated in the 1930s and 1940s, but his most celebrated single contribution to this field appeared in a journal article published in 1917. Hence, we are again dealing with a longstanding interest, in which persistent central ideas appear and reappear, usually in increasingly systematic form. Clark's interests in overhead costs, and in forging a workably competitive economy, also tie in directly with his concerns with the cycle, stabilization, and full employment. The connection between overhead costs and the accelerator has already been observed; the tie between full employment policy and wage-price relationships will shortly be noted.

APPROACH TO THE BUSINESS CYCLE

Clark's approach to the study of the business cycle was strictly pragmatic. He wanted to isolate those factors in the business cycle which seem to have the greatest strategic importance, and to focus on these. Further, he defined strategic importance as having real power to control other factors and to determine the nature of the result. Finally, he assigned peculiar strategic importance to those factors over which we have at least potential power of control.

In his listing of such peculiarly strategic factors, Clark gave first position to a phenomenon he had isolated formally as early as 1917, and to which he had alluded even earlier. This was the tendency toward intensified fluctuations of derived demand for durable goods. This tendency included both capital equipment and consumers' goods, although especially the former, with lesser like tendencies for raw materials. Clark labeled this factor "of basic importance," not only to the cycle but also to stabilization efforts. If this tendency could be controlled, a great stabilization of the average rate of productive activity could be achieved; as a secondary result, consumers' expenditures could be far more stable. This leads us, of course, to a brief recall of Clark's technical contribution relating to this strategic factor—the "accelerator" or, perhaps more properly, the "acceleration principle."

THE ACCELERATOR

This concept, first formally developed by Clark in 1917, also reappeared in its full business-cycle context in Clark's two cycle-relevant books of the 1930s. As early as 1917, however, Clark noted some peculiar properties of this behavior of derived demand. This behavior acts as an intensifier of the disturbances it transmits, but it can also produce a diminution of demand on its own. It can parlay a diminishing rate of growth in one industry into an absolute decline in another. This rests basically upon technical necessities—upon the way "the demand for finished products is handed on in the form of a demand for machines, tools, construction materials, and unfinished goods in general" (PSE, p. 328).

The key 1917 article includes a summary of the findings of the paper that is so precise and incisive as to defy paraphrasing:

> In summary, the chief attempt of this study has been to give an exact formulation to the relationship, in quantity and in time, between demand for products and demand for the means of production; a relationship which plays a large part in several different theories of business cycles, and the results of which are so obvious that almost all descriptions of business cycles display them. The main principles contended for are as follows:
> 1.   The demand for enlarging the means of production (including stocks of finished goods on the way to the consumer) varies, not with the volume of the demand for the finished product, but rather with the acceleration of that demand, allowance being made for the fact that the equipment cannot be adjusted as rapidly as demand changes, and so may be unusually scarce or redundant to start with in any given period. The demand for equipment may decrease as a result of this law even though the demand for the finished product is still growing.
> 2.   The total demand for producers' goods tends to vary more sharply than the demand for finished products, the intensification being in proportion to the average life of the goods in question.
> 3.   The maximum and minimum points in the demand for producers' goods tend to precede the maximum and minimum points in the demand for the finished products, the effect being that the change may appear to precede its own cause. (PSE, p. 348)

J.M. Clark continued to work on the acceleration concept, and to clarify, refine, and delimit his version. Additional aspects are developed in *Studies in the Economics of Overhead Costs* (1923), and especially in *Strategic Factors in Business Cycles* (1934), which contains his most comprehensive reworking. His elaborations and sharpening came partly as a result of the drift of his own work, and doubtless in part as a consequence of penetrating exchanges with Ragnar Frisch and later Simon Kuznets, who put the concept to a statistical test.

Clark, in an "Additional Note" appended to the 1936 reprint of the 1917 article, sees the principal extension of the concept which he made in *Strategic Factors in Business Cycles* as "the application of the theory to durable goods in general." He recalls: "and emphasis was laid on the way in which the effect of changes in activity in the durable-goods industries returns upon general consumer-demand, and so on, in a theoretically endless series of cycles. Thus the originating movement (which *may* occur at any point in the system) tends to be overlaid by these after-effects, so that its original character cannot be traced statistically" (PSE, p. 349). This latter point is important to his dispute with Kuznets.

In the course of answering Kuznets, he sheds further light on the acceleration principle as an abstraction or model.

These citations may serve to show how the hypothesis in question was intended to be used. If taken as a picture of what must happen in real life, it would involve the absurd condition that producers of finished goods never have any excess or shortage of capacity (except when demand has shrunk faster than productive equipment can shrink by wearing out), while producers of productive equipment have always enough excess capacity to handle instantly any demand that may be put upon them. There is, of course, no reason for supposing that these two groups of producers behave in such diametrically opposite ways. Actually, each group has normally some excess capacity, part of which at least is likely to be of inferior quality and worth replacing or modernising if it comes into more constant demand. In respect to this and other matters Dr. Kuznets has contributed so substantially to elaborating the necessary qualifications and modifications of this provisional hypothesis that it causes some surprise to see him reverting to it to apply his statistical test and setting up as my theory what I had called "the impossibly fluid condition of industry that was previously assumed." (PSE, p. 351)

The acceleration principle has limits, as Frisch, Kuznets, and subsequent writers have made clear. It has been noted that the presumed response in the output of capital goods as a result of changes in the level of consumer demand assumes no other way of increasing output—in short, it assumes full employment of resources. The holding of large inventories might also muffle the acceleration effect. Others have suggested that innovations might cause spurts in investment that could not be explained in terms of immediate consumer demand. These and other limitations in the precise applicability of the acceleration principle do not, however, invalidate the basic concept.

As with the concept of overhead costs, Clark did not "invent" the idea that he labeled the acceleration principle. This insight can be found in crude form in many nineteenth- and early twentieth-century writings. Such writers as Spiethoff, Pigou, Harrod, Carver, and especially Aftalion dealt with the idea, but Seligman concludes "it remained for Clark to make it central to the explanation of cycles, where it was pictured as the key element in a self-generating process." J. R. Hicks adds that when the mathematical possibilities of the acceleration principle were noted by Frisch and others, the principle entered the mainstream of macroeconomics. In this process, what Hicks terms the "economic intuition" of Clark, and his persistence in defending his insight, played an important role. In 1962, when the *Journal of Political Economy* celebrated its seventieth anniversary by assembling into a book 24 articles deemed to be the most original and seminal appearing in the first seventy volumes, Clark's 1917 paper on "Business Acceleration and the Law of Demand" was included.

Clark also contributed to the other half of the accelerator-multiplier component of modern macro theory. In his 1931 book *The Costs of the World War to the American People*, Clark expounds a rough but clearly identifiable foreign-trade multiplier. In his *Economics of Planning Public Works* (1935), and (more widely known) in his *Strategic Factors in Business Cycles* (1934), his version of the multiplier is extended and refined. Clark saw early that there would be leakages over time. He wrote: "If a reduction of production, and of income, is followed by a *smaller* reduction of expenditures, then the series of derived effects is a dwindling series of the type which should have a finite, not an infinite sum" (SF, p. 85). Likewise, the effects of an increase in income are finite and are limited to a relatively short period of time.

STABILIZATION AND FULL EMPLOYMENT POLICY

Clark's concern with business cycle theory was always as the physiology necessary to a subsequent prescription of medicine. He was interested in effective control of the wilder oscillations of the business cycle, and in reasonably full employment, and he knew that understanding of causes was a means to that end.

Clark's early conviction that much of this stabilization, especially regularization of employment, could be accomplished by actions of industry never completely disappeared. Beginning in 1926, however, his emphasis shifted firmly toward what the larger society, through government, could also do. His preferences were always for mild rather than drastic measures; for indirect instead of direct controls; and for action that would complement rather than supersede or negate the efforts of the private sector. Yet, he was advocating by the early 1930s policies clearly in anticipation of Keynes, and in subsequent years he apparently grew increasingly comfortable with the macroeconomic policy. He never, however, became reconciled to the idea of permanent pump-priming per se, nor to the possibility of perpetual deficit spending.

He was able by 1949 to join (although he had reservations shortly to be noted) other members of a "Group of Experts" asked to recommend to the United Nations appropriate macroeconomic policy instruments. Their report included recommendations that each government should adopt and announce a full employment target; announce its program for coordinating its fiscal and monetary policies, investment and production planning, and wage and price policies toward that full employment target; adopt and announce appropriate compensatory measures designed to expand effective demand and to be triggered automatically; announce the nature of its price-stabilization policies; and adapt its legislative, administrative, and statistical procedures to the implementation of its full-employment program.

Clark had also become, long before that time, an authority on the economics of planning public works. His study made for the National Planning Board in 1935, *Economics of Planning Public Works*, remains to this date what Sumner Slichter maintained it to be when he reviewed the study: "the best book available" in this field. In this short book he discusses the several purposes of public works, the nature of the economic dislocations they are to counteract, alternative timing policies, net effects, nullifying factors, problems encountered, and myriad other matters.

All of this was laced with a pervasive caution and skepticism, for although Clark was constructive and a craftsman bent on improving this policy, he had few illusions. He concluded that "The amount of public works which could, within reason, be concentrated in dull times, does not appear from the figures as likely to be large enough, by itself, to counteract even a moderate depression. Such a policy could succeed only as part of a much larger program" (SF, pp. 198–99).

Although Clark concurred in the Report of the UN Special Group, he also issued a separate statement emphasizing the importance of another aspect of full employment policy. This is the development of an appropriate wage-price policy that will further, or at least not impede or negate, the main thrust of the otherwise predominantly macroeconomic policy advocated in this Report. While acknowledging that this is "no man's land" in which we do not have the requisite theory or understanding, he argues strongly that this problem is relevant enough to warrant intensive study and troubling enough to preclude overconfidence as to the effectiveness of simplistic macro policy. In his separate statement, which is quite short, he gives examples designed to demonstrate that while the wage-price structure will neither cause nor cure mass unemployment, it can bear materially on the effectiveness of full employment policy. He concludes:

With an unfavorable structure, it may be impossible to set as high an employment target as with a favourable structure or it may be possible only at the cost of price inflation, or an increase in the burden of public debt, or both. Improvements in the structure may be necessary for attaining a fully satisfactory employment-target; and in countries attaching importance to voluntary methods, this may take time. (UN, pp. 102–3)

As he stated, adequate and stable job opportunity rests on two, not one, main conditions: adequate effective demand, and a wage-price system that will make it possible for this effective demand to be translated into production and employment rather than into inflation of money costs and restriction in output.

Some opponents of macro full-employment policy have taken this addendum to the Special Group report to be a repudiation of the main macro thrust of the document. A careful reading of

Clark's "separate concurring statement" does not validate this interpretation. Not only did Clark concur in the main report, he reiterates in his own statement that although he believes appropriate cost-price structures to be a coordinate goal, he agrees entirely that fiscal policy is of dominant importance in stabilizing cyclical fluctuations and of major importance in maintaining high levels of long-run income and employment. He does add, characteristically, that he lacks total confidence in the ability of this policy to maintain any desired level of national income under any and all conditions.

Gottfried Haberler, in reading what he terms Clark's "cautious remarks" in this addendum, states that his own attitude of caution is strengthened in the reading. William J. Fellner, in the first AEA *Survey* volume, confirms Clark's estimate that this relationship between cost-price problems and the level of employment remains largely unexplored, although Ellis, Haberler, and others have joined Clark in noting the relevance of the problem. Fellner explains this vacuum by suggesting that the problem of the effects of cost-price policies is inherently more complicated than that of the effects of conventional macro policy.

◀ 3 ▶

The Economics of Welfare

J. M. Clark was deeply and pervasively concerned with the attainment of economic welfare, defined in broad and long-run terms. This welfare, he contended, would not eventuate wholly or perhaps even largely from the choices and strivings of men and women acting as isolated agents or atomistic particles. Welfare, and the realization of social values, would operate within the broad framework of social control.

SOCIAL CONTROL

The nature, extent, and legitimization of that social control constituted another of the themes with which Clark remained concerned over most of his half century of professional activity. The public came to know his position through two editions of his famous book, *Social Control of Business*, appearing in 1926 and in 1939. The profession knew, of course, that his interests both predated and postdated these editions, and that his focus upon social control encompassed far more than social control of business alone. In the first edition, he sketched his central concept of social control in these terms:

> "Social control" is control exercised by the entity we call "society." But society never acts as whole; it never even makes decisions as a unit, much less puts them into effect. The most definite and powerful agent of society is government, and in this country the municipal, state, and federal governments between them exercise the formal, legal power of control in economic life. But social control is wider than this, as we have already seen. One's newspaper, one's trade union or professional association or chamber of commerce, one's neighbors, one's church, all exercise some measure of social control. . . .
> Since none of our actual organizations takes in everybody who is concerned, social control as we have it is always exercised on behalf of a particular group, something less than the sum of all the human beings who have vital interests at stake. In a broad sense, we may call it social control whenever the individual is forced or persuaded to act in the interest of any group of which he is a member, rather than in his own personal interest. In this sense the nation exercises control, but so also does the trade union. (SC, p. 8)

Clark found some sort of control by society of the economic actions of persons or groups virtually coexistent with human history. The doctrine of complete individualism he found to have been fleeting, localized, and never fully realized in practice. For free (and uncontrolled) enterprise to function effectively would require a degree of knowledge, capacity, autonomy, and competition on the part of individuals that has not yet been attained. If any of these conditions are not present, Clark asserted, corrective measures by society are warranted even on the basis of nineteenth-century utilitarianism.

The rough approximization of laissez-faire that prevailed in some places during part of the nineteenth century fostered, or at least did not prevent, amazing material gains. These gains gave rise to the hope that progress could continue indefinitely, automatically, and within an institutional framework that needed only maintenance, not drastic repair or change. It is now apparent, concluded Clark, this age was one of transition, technologically and institutionally. Clark noted, in the fateful year 1929:

> To sum up the changes which have come about in the century and a half since the gospel of individualism gained its first great vogue, one may say that the economic world is no longer an arithmetic sum of independent personal interests wherein each may look out for his own and the aggregate will thus be best promoted. It has become again a consciously interdependent organism as it was in the middle ages, but on a far vaster scale with a far greater complexity of interests to be adjusted by standards and methods which can borrow little from the medieval experience but must be worked out afresh. (GC, p. 75)

In this new kind of world, the public stake in the behavior of industry is not sufficiently safeguarded by the institutions of individualism. Society has the right to interfere, where it sees its interests clearly contravened and when it can develop adequate and efficient means to promote them.

Clark issued this manifesto: "To sum up, social control must reckon with the forces of supply and demand but does not stand helpless before them" (SC, p. 459). He observed that if society wishes to raise the wages of ditch diggers, it has many means at its disposal. It can diminish the supply of ditch diggers by reducing barriers to higher-paid jobs; it can raise wages at least until positive violence is done to market equilibrium; it can experiment to determine what rate will be tolerated by supply and demand; and it may use methods other than reliance on natural market forces, if circumstances dictate. Such methods may be "crude, difficult, not wholly to be relied on, but they may suffice if there are really great evils to be prevented and urgent needs to be met."

Clark's concept of social control, and his delineation of complete free enterprise as largely an ephemeral ideology, may well now seem trite to some. In the decades during which Clark did his classic work in this field it was by no means commonplace or obvious. Whether he influenced the course of events by enunciating what Karl Mannheim would term a utopian vision, or whether he was simply observing the already evident tide of history, may remain moot, although he would surely have opted for the latter role.

WELFARE ECONOMICS

Clark believed that the rise of a separate subdiscipline termed "welfare economics" reflects the increasingly self-conscious desire of economics to separate its analysis of what is from its judgments of what ought to be. A. C. Pigou, in his *Wealth and Welfare*, published in 1912, postulated an "unverified probability" that welfare would be increased by a larger national dividend, by a more equalitarian distribution (unless this lowered output too much), and by greater stability. He also suggested a form of social accounting that might help to identify instances in which a given added use of resources would add either a greater or lesser amount to the national dividend than to the income of the person making the outlay.

John A. Hobson, two years later, based his version of welfare economics on John Ruskin's "There is no wealth but life." Hobson did not attempt to restrict his concern to economic welfare alone, but asked, "What is welfare, and how is it affected by existing methods of producing and circulating wealth?" He found welfare to be an organic whole, not an aggregation of marginal units of satisfaction. Hobson was disregarded by the profession as nonscientific. Clark adds, however:

> If Hobson's welfare economics left the scientific economics out, the form of theory which now bears the name can without real unfairness be described as welfare economics with the welfare left out, in a remarkably resolute attempt to meet the real or supposed requirements of economic science. Rejecting "interpersonal comparisons," this body of theory seems to end in rather complete agnosticism, aside from policies that increase the national dividend without making anyone worse off. But the existence of a single disadvantaged person acts as a veto on scientific approval of any policy—one cannot be scientifically certain that his loss does not outweigh the gains of many. . . . It seems clear that this theory has not reached satisfactory final form. (EI, p. 59)

Contemporary welfare economics, Clark notes, places special

emphasis on employing only criteria that can pass muster as scientific and cannot be stigmatized as representing the writer's own "value judgments." This approach leads to accepting people's desires as they are, and trying to determine how well the system furthers their realization. Clark sees in this contemporary drift a strong desire both to make welfare judgments and to attach the label of "science" and "objective inquiry" to them. The welfare judgments need objective evidence and analysis as rationale; the inquiry needs a tie to social and moral purposes.

CLARK'S CONCEPT OF WELFARE

While Clark was more interested in isolating and protecting the values that are usually accepted as *elements* of welfare than he was in a neat theoretical model of the system he nevertheless felt constrained to sketch the general conception of welfare that pervades much of the vast bulk of his writing. He summarizes this concept:

Welfare is here conceived in terms of needs, rather than of an undiscriminating list of desires. It calls for healthy and responsible individuals, organized in a healthy society which in turn is responsible to and for its members. To inquire into needs, as distinct from desires, implies that somebody can distinguish between them; that is, that society can command specialized knowledge or wisdom, or both, which has a validity superior to the uninstructed choices of all or most of its unspecialized members. Such knowledge is available, for a growing number of purposes. Even the best of us can benefit by the advice of specialists —though we do not always act in accord even with our own maturer judgment of our own welfare or of that of society. (EI, p. 116)

This concept very quickly leads beyond the marketplace. The necessary search for standards of social value in the economic world is an enormously difficult but potentially very rewarding task. We probably cannot find a measure of social value as tangible and manageable as the dollar yardstick. Yet, Clark argues, we may discover standards that can serve to modify or even in some cases to replace market evaluations, if we are willing to accept three fundamental propositions.

One of these propositions is that the collective efficiency of private enterprise involves quantities and qualities of which actual market prices may not be the only measure, or which may command no market price at all under prevailing institutional arrangements. A second is that although nonmarket measures of value are almost certainly less exact than those of the market, they may also be much more fundamental. A third is that our guiding standards should not be dependent upon prevailing institutions of private competitive exchange, but should be capable of holding even under socialism.

Clark asks: "Does anyone really accept the scale of the competitive market? We shall have found such a man, when we have found one who honestly approves of existing conditions of poverty: not one who is resigned to them as an inevitable evil, but one who would not lessen them if he could. So long as this does not represent the prevailing sentiment, so long it will be impossible to say that market value measures 'social value' in the sense of 'value to society' " (PSE, p. 50).

Part of the reason for daring to venture beyond the market is that "unpaid costs and unappropriated services" abound in the world. As a society approaches affluence, such intangible utilities as knowledge and personal privacy loom larger. In a democratic society, people are also torn by two contradictory social impulses: to be like others, and to be different from them. But, Clark observes, these "emulative and especially these invidious utilities are in a peculiar way the ones in which one man's gain must be another's loss: they eat each other up, and the resultant is a social utility far different from the sum of the individually appropriable parts." (PSE, p. 46)

"DIFFUSED GAINS AND COSTS"

Clark very early revealed a perceptive understanding of what he termed "diffused gains and costs," and which we might recognize as externalities or as social costs or benefits. He admitted that this term encompasses a motley array of cases, united only "by the common fact that net financial income realizable by private enterprise is an inaccurate measure of total net contribution to economic values."

In most cases these diffused effects can be isolated and identified; and some are potentially measurable, although currently they seldom actually are measured. The problem of taking adequate account of these social gains and losses would be just as acute in a collectivist society as in our own: it is a pervasive problem with no guarantees of a correct answer.

Under a system of private enterprise, diffused gains (or externalities) might induce the public to undertake some kinds of production that would not "pay off" for private enterprise. Inducements by communities, designed to attract industry, or such activities as the TVA, are cases in point. In making a social evaluation of such projects, the key question is whether they create production that would not otherwise take place or merely determine the location of production, which in any case would have to take place somewhere. Uncompensated diffused losses, or social costs, have led to accepted kinds of preventive controls, such as land zoning and abatement of stream or air pollution.

Although Clark's basic position is as relevant, and far more widely accepted, now than it was in 1916 (when he first fully articulated much of it) the locus of responsibility does not seem nearly so limited to us as it did to Clark. Although he acknowledged from the outset the necessity of broader governmental action, as well as acceptance by industry of greater social responsibility, he tended during much of his professional career to opt for the latter. He wrote in 1926:

Every honest business man wants to pay his debts, to meet his money liabilities. If he does this, he is self-supporting. But these money liabilities are only the rather imperfect representatives of the ultimate costs incurred and damages inflicted in the operation of the industry, and the business is not really self-supporting unless it compensates all these ultimate costs and damages, and compensates them adequately. In other words, the simple morality of self-support must be given a vastly enlarged interpretation, and extended into fields where its requirements cannot easily be defined.

For instance, no business is self-sustaining unless it takes care of its fair quota of the costs of unemployment: the idleness occasioned by its own operations. . . . This same need would be met in a more positive way if it should ever come to pass that industry should regard as its main business the furnishing of worth-while conditions of work and opportunities for worth-while life to the people who get their living out of it. (SC, pp. 242–43.)

Later in his career, while never relinquishing his position that industry should accept broad social responsibilities as a major participating member in a system of voluntary pluralism, Clark tended to emphasize broader social judgments, made through government, about diffused gains and costs. He noted that when economists engage in practical thinking on matters of public policy, they do take these matters into account. When an economist supports an ordinance limiting the height of buildings he is applying the "theory of unpaid costs." When he votes to subsidize a railroad entering virgin territory, he is paying for "inappropriable services." When he recommends a minimum wage law, he is making a social estimate of the value of a certain level of living for the poor—an estimate the market might not make. Social insurance, free public education, and other elements in what Clark terms "the social minimum" further reflect the willingness and indeed the determination of society to make social judgments of this sort.

Clark makes the further observation, obviously alluding to the professed inability of modern "welfare economists" to make interpersonal comparisons of satisfaction, that society has long since made a rough but firm judgment in this sector:

It seems that, while theory has not been able to reach an uncontested decision as to the relative individual utility of goods to richer and poorer individuals, democratic judgments have sustained the social minimum largely on different grounds—as a means to individuals' appropriate participation in the common life. Their needs, from this standpoint, are a basis of claims of 'rights,' which are less elusive than their relative capacities for enjoyment and furnish a more solid ground for policy. (EI, p. 66)

THE WELFARE OF MAN OR MACHINE?

Clark placed great emphasis throughout his career upon the importance, and the influence, of machine technology.

Without accepting the machine mystique of Veblen, he nevertheless consistently related capital-intensive industrial technology to
the problems of maintaining competition, stabilizing the business
cycle, and gaining recognition of social values. In the latter case,
as in the earlier instances, the interests of man and the machine
may not be wholly the same. In an eloquent statement made in
1922, Clark has a Kafka-like vision of how these interests may
clash, to the detriment of man's welfare:

Ride through the industrial district stretching from South Chicago to
Gary, and as you view the expanse of ugly flats and barrens, ask yourself
why these people are here. Is this a place men would choose to live in?
Certainly not, if they were free to move out to those blue, wooded hills
beckoning in the distance. These people never wanted to live here. But
the machines did, and that settled it. If you wish to see who it was that
found this site desirable, look yonder at that row of pot-bellied Titans
with their grotesquely sprawling limbs, squatting near a feed-trough that
looks at least a quarter of a mile in length. Behold, my friends, the only
beings who actually wanted to live here, out of a total population of a
hundred thousand people and six blast furnaces! The rest are here because the furnaces are here and for no other reason. They either were
bribed or came under duress of earning their bread, to this place of
dreary flatness where there seems no soil wherein the soul of man may
strike its roots. Nor is this an isolated case. From Homestead to Hol-
lywood the machines have reared cities after their own needs, the like of
which man never saw before.
The machines originally made bargains with man, in which they
offered him things he much desired, and in exchange bound him to serve
and maintain them, to eliminate the unfit among them and promote their
racial progress, and to alter his own social and political arrangements in
whatever ways might be necessary in keeping pace with the increasingly
complex social organization of the machines themselves, and in keeping
the children of man faithful to the service the machines require. The full
nature of the terms of these bargains was not, however, revealed to man
at the first. Some of the terms became evident only after generations had
passed, and of some we cannot yet be sure. (EM, p. 136)

VOLUNTARY PLURALISM

Clark saw the United States as a true pluralistic society. Although he envisaged social control as pervasive and inescapable, he hoped that this control would be largely effected by

the voluntary cooperation of the major groups in the society. A chapter heading in *Alternative to Serfdom*, "Toward a Society of Responsible Individuals in Responsible Groups," indicates his own aspiration for our economy.

Public controls, in the form of democratic planning, regulation, and establishment of ground rules, seem clearly preferable to public ownership and operation. Clark conceded that governmental operation may be needed in industries whose stimulation is undesirable, or where private enterprise is not willing to function, or as a means of providing necessary service without profit, or where public ownership of some units may help to regulate rates or prices of competing private units. Nevertheless, Clark's clear preference was for public control rather than public ownership.

The form of that control, however, should be as democratic, noncoercive, and perhaps indirect as possible. It should also enlist the consent, cooperation, and participation of the major groups in the economy. Clark refers to the contention of many that all economic legislation is "socialistic," and he notes the position taken by some that only two conditions are possible—complete individualism or complete socialization—with no logical or workable stopping point in between. This position he rejects:

> As over against this I would suggest another statement as containing, on the whole, more truth—namely, two conditions are impossible: pure individualism and complete socialism. Everything practicable lies in the realm between, bare of logical anchorages though it may be. There has always been more control than the theory of pure individualism calls for, for the practice has never followed the theory. And one may hazard that, save for brief experiments or small communities there will always be a large and important place for the principle of free voluntary action and of mutual arrangements for the mutual advantage of those immediately and primarily concerned. (GC, p. 75)

When Clark uses the term "responsible" or "responsibility," he gives it a twofold meaning. The term implies a range of choices and discretion for the individual, which he views with due regard for the rights of others; it also implies accountability to others for the use that is made of this discretion. This stops short of pure altruism, and Clark believes it to be achievable even in "our turbulent society." Achievable or not, it is judged to be better than the alternatives—centralized collectivism, decentralized collectivism, or (perhaps most radical of all) an attempt to actually establish perfect competition. The only possible system for this society, he believes, is what some call a mixed system, or as he prefers to term it a "balanced" system.

For nearly two centuries, he argues, we have sought an illusory society in which irresponsible self-interest would organize a community in which men could live in dignity and harmony. We have trusted either to the mechanical functioning of the market, or to a politics amoral and insensitive to community need. The needs we have neglected in the process can be met only in part by the state. In large part they must be promoted by groups, sometimes competing and sometimes collaborating, with a recognition of the social stake in their interaction. Clark added, however, a vital proviso: an adequate balance of power among these groups. This means, of course, that every individual is not free to dictate or to choose how far social control shall go:

So this requires him to accept voluntarily a collective decision that will seldom draw the line precisely where he would have chosen to draw it. He will force the line to be drawn too far on the side of regimentation unless, in many matters, he limits his liberty without waiting for law to do it for him. And the principles guiding such limitation, while easy to accept in the abstract, are very difficult to apply to concrete cases, especially one's own case. Those who have new rights to conquer cannot easily visualize the duties that go with them, or even the fact that new rights carry new duties and are forfeit otherwise. Still harder to realize are the dangers of power without adequate social purpose. When all these requirements have been measurably met, we can claim to be an economic community. (AS, p. 152)

This emphasis on "voluntary pluralism," operating through a democratic government, seems bland and overly sanguine to contemporary men. To those who doubt the responsibility of the parties, their willingness to compete as well as to collude, their rough parity or balance in bargaining strength, or their legitimacy as quasi-government, this approach seems neither tough enough nor realistic enough. The approach is not out of harmony with Galbraith's early concept of countervailing power, nor with

Boulding's "organizational revolution," nor with Berle's "conscience of the king." It does come in jarring juxtaposition, however, with the "power elite" of Mills, the "organization man" of Whyte, or the technostructure and dominance of corporate planning found in the latter-day Galbraith.

Even to some friendly critics, the voluntary pluralism or "social economy in moderation" of Clark seem somehow to be in a political vacuum, or at least to envisage a milder, gentler, social and political order than we actually have. Alan T. Peacock, in his review (see Bibliography) of Clark's *Alternative to Serfdom* concludes:

He does make a courageous attempt to solve the problem of conflict between strong groups inimical to economic well-being and ultimately to stable government while recognising the necessity of retaining them as the important decision-making units in the economic system. But while it is always timely to remind us that with the acquisition of new rights, particularly those guaranteed by the state, new duties, often difficult to visualise, go with them, Professor Clark shrinks from any discussion of the appropriate political milieu in which the process of mutual understanding is to be developed. It is obvious that he has some difficulty in steering a course between the "dangers" of the corporatist and competitive "solutions," and while one may agree with Professor Clark that the speed of advance towards solving the tremendous problems presented by group organisation must necessarily be slow, one can never be sure of the ultimate direction that he has in mind. (p. 119)

Robert S. Lynd, in his review (see Bibliography) of the same book, goes still further. Clark is said to lack a dynamic or realistic theory of group membership and action. He treats major groups as though they were voluntary associations, hoping to get from them a "balanced society." He does not confront the "primary massive grouping of our society into classes" and the antagonisms and coercions this involves. The reviewer continues, "even so perceptive an economist as Professor Clark lacks any realistic awareness of the dynamics of power in our type of society. He writes as though classes can turn on and off their use of power like a spiggot." Again, "[Clark] has not, I believe, faced the positive potentialities of collective social action. . . . his imagination simply goes dead before collectivism." The reviewer recalls a note appearing in an English publication upon the death of Keynes, which observed that Keynes was "an optimist who always hoped that businessmen would do that which they did not in fact do." The reviewer concludes that this remark also applies to Professor Clark. It is perhaps fair to say that Clark's diagnosis of our society, and even his prognosis as to its future, have received much wider support than has his confidence in a halfway house of moderation.

◄4►

Economics as a Discipline

Clark was continually concerned with the scope, nature, and methods of economics, although he was wryly aware of how pretentious (and contentious) pronouncements on such matters can be. The term "methodology" seldom if ever appears in his writing, but in a broad sense that pedantic term applies to many persistent threads in his thinking. He loved his discipline, but he was concerned about it, too; and he was capable of gently (and sometimes not so gently) chiding it for its wayward ways. He also epitomized, in his writings and in his person, a stance, a method, a position about what economics should be doing and how it might go about it. In this section of the essay, both his writings and his example will be invoked.

SCOPE AND BOUNDARIES OF ECONOMICS

In a piece on professors, notably economics professors, Clark makes clear his feelings that academic economics is far too concerned with maintaining the security of its borders and too little concerned with following problems across those borders. This leads many, he adds,

> to adjudge it unscientific to consider the human importance of things and to ask what ends economic mechanisms serve—the only scientific method being to accept as final data the choices made by individuals, mainly or entirely the kind of choices made in markets. In particular, there is the school which insists that economists must make no "interpersonal comparisons" of values, and there is the "welfare economics," built within this strange self-imposed restriction, which means in effect that it must accept the kinds of valuations—including interpersonal comparisons—which markets make. The notorious social biases of such choices are not cured by the fact that other practically-available ways of reaching decisions are also biased. (SCC, p. 9)

Clark cheerfully acknowledges, however, that the special services of "the guild" in developing tools and refining theory are not to be underestimated. Professors of economics seem to be positively useful on occasion—but, he believes, that usefulness is enhanced when they serve as members of a balanced team. In a later statement, Clark reiterates and extends this theme:

> We must defend the right of free academic inquiry. . . . Its job includes exploring what may ultimately prove to have been blind alleys; but it also includes freedom for those who think the alleys *are* blind, to search for more promising routes. We must speak, and work, for the cooperation between disciplines, and between academic and nonacademic thinking, which may broaden economic perspectives and bring economics into working relation with more realistic concepts of welfare. If there is truth in the saying that war is too important to be left to generals, or that public finance is too important to be left to financiers, there may be some of the same kind of truth in the proposition that economics, where it becomes involved with welfare, is too important to be left at the exclusive mercy of economists. (EI, pp. 168–69)

In a prophetic essay entitled "The Interpenetration of Politics and Economics," (EI) as well as on other occasions, Clark makes a special point of the necessity for collaboration between economists and political scientists. Increasingly, governmental action is deeply influencing and even shaping the economy. Yet, concurrently, such nominally economic institutions as the massive corporation or the large labor union have not only become political bodies internally but are now also an important part of the quasi-public, quasi-private apparatus of government. Neither economics nor political science can function fully without an intellectual interpenetration comparable to that occurring in our actual society. Out of this may come a genuine political economy.

"What, then," asks Clark, "are the proper boundaries of economic science? Unless they have been finally and authoritatively established in some writing which has escaped my notice, I feel free to contend that it is less important to keep inside any traditional limits than to follow our natural questionings wherever they may lead, and do whatever work we are specially fitted for and find undone." (PSE, p. 60)

This willingness to follow questions wherever they may lead, whether strictly within the bounds of economics or not, is reflected not only in his writing, as the Bibliography attests, but in the evolution of his own thinking. He could learn from orthodoxy, especially from J. B. Clark; he could learn from the "heretics" Veblen and Hobson; and he could learn from the psychologist James or the sociologist Cooley. His was not a world of neat compartments and disciplinary barricades.

STATICS AND DYNAMICS

Should economics focus primarily upon statics, or upon dynamics? Clark's answer was, of course, "upon both." He did believe, however, that the economics his generation had inherited (and which persisted) was much more nearly complete in its static than in its dynamic analysis. He addressed himself during much of his long productive lifetime to redressing that balance: in price theory, in macroeconomics, and in helping to formulate a broader and more fundamental concept of welfare.

Clark believed that insofar as dynamic conditions contrast with static in "mechanical" ways only, static findings may be made dynamic by quantitative adjustments. But if the differences are qualitative or "chemical" in nature (to utilize the word employed by J. S. Mill), heterodox methods and new inductions may be in order. He believed that in many cases in which static premises differ from assumptions proper to dynamics, the differences are indeed "chemical"—as in the dynamic character of human nature and the evolving path of institutions. Clark observes:

> The key to statics, as we have seen, is a problem: that of levels of equilibrium. This is an abstraction based on observation of the relative stability of economic values, and of oscillations whose behavior suggests a normal level toward which the economic forces of gravity exert their pull. The key to dynamics is a different problem: that of processes which do not visibly tend to any complete and definable static equilibrium. The importance of this shift from the search for levels to the study of processes can hardly be overemphasized; it is not less significant than the change from static to dynamic conditions. (PSE, p. 203)

If dynamics must rely largely on new inductions and premises, will anything be left of statics? Clark answered that at least three claims to usefulness would remain. First, dynamics will never solve or even structure all of its problems, and even provisional static answers will remain the best we have. Second, in such fields as price levels, statics can be fruitfully adapted by quantitative modifications of static formulas. Third, much of the emerging dynamics will find it necessary to refer to the parallel static literature for comparison and checkpoint.

To the plaint that he did not understand that static theory proclaims its own limitations, he has a tart answer:

> Professor Fetter claims that I do not understand static theory in that static theory emphasizes its own limitations. Nobody realizes more clearly than I do that as compared to theory which is unconsciously static, any theory which announces its static character takes a long step in the right direction. But a sign which announces: "This happy valley is not the whole world" does not take the place of explorations outside the happy valley, no matter how many exclamation points there are on the sign." (*American Economic Review*, 9:323, March 1919)

INDUCTION OR DEDUCTION?

Clark's answer, once again, would be "both." As a theorist of competence and stature, even if one not overly fond of formal models of the traditional type, he would not reject deduction—indeed he defended it. Yet, as a man eager to develop dynamic economics of a fundamental sort, and to restore economics to the world of reality as well as thought, empirical work seemed imperative. Hence, in his writing about method, and in his own work, penetrating deductive flights (albeit using "descriptive analysis" rather than mathematical models) are joined to thorough, systematic, and rigorous use of data, in the most scrupulous and meticulous of studies of particular problems.

Much of the discredit attached to the deductive method can be traced, he believed, to the attempts of many economists (notably of the nineteenth-century classical school and its descendents) to construe it as leading to ultimate truth. They were too confident that their assumptions covered all the facts, and that their results were universally applicable economic laws. Used less pretentiously, Clark argued, deductive study yielded insightful and useful results that a contemporary economist cannot do without:

> General economics must simplify in order to interpret; otherwise its description will be just as unwieldy and baffling as the world itself. Thus theoretical economics must steer a course somewhere between what is futile and what is impossible. It will be a never-ending search for generalizations that are significantly true, and for that very reason are often neither one hundred per cent accurate, nor universally applicable. (PSE, p. 10)

An antidote to any complacency regarding the adequacy of either deduction or induction, taken by itself, is provided by the sociology of knowledge, which holds that the purest of thought is "existentially conditioned." Clark himself, in his classic study of Adam Smith, makes this point with force:

> To understand such thought we must take into account the conditions of the time and what went before; to select from it the elements of value for our own use we must see it in relation to what has come after and to

the changed conditions which now prevail. For the first purpose we must view Adam Smith in relation to an age in which factories were tiny, the machine was still hardly more than a machine tool, the competitive system was young and struggling against eighteenth-century mercantilism and survivals of medieval restrictions which had outlived their function. For present purposes we must view Smith's individualism in the light of such facts as railroads, holding-companies, centralized banking, business barometrics and giant power. The teleology of his "unseen hand" must be appraised in terms of Darwinism; its optimism in the light of modern psychiatry. Specific doctrines will be discredited, yet something, perhaps of more value, will remain. (PSE, p. 171)

Although J. M. Clark denied any basic conflict, either in theory and methods, between his work and that of his father, there was surely often a striking difference in emphasis—in this case, as to the means of arriving at theory. T. Suranyi-Unger, in *Economics in the Twentieth Century*, (see Bibliography) has sketched this contrast:

The other, much more important, reform movement in American economic theory can perhaps be best illustrated by a parallelism between the older and the younger Clark. The former belongs to that great generation of American economists who, full of enthusiasm for the scientific ideals borrowed from Germany, founded the American Economic Association in 1886 and, without having published much previously, without material means, and without important academic chairs, determined to breathe a new spirit into the economic theory of their country. This bold attempt was crowned with success, and in a few years they had everywhere conquered: through them American economics entered upon its classical age. The older Clark is at the head of this movement. He considered the widest perspectives of economic phenomena, dealt with them from the deductive side and produced thereby a pleasing, optimistic, and abstract-deductive system. His son, who entered upon his scientific career with the purpose of further developing his father's thoughts, could not free himself from the influence of a new tendency which had meanwhile arisen and had to admit that economic theory should be based on the results of the "new psychology." The first quarter of the twentieth century begins in American economics with the great work on distribution of the older Clark, and closes with his son's work on the theory of production, which is perhaps of no less importance. The great change which has taken place since then in the science of the new world, is clearly reflected in the general spirit of these two books. At the present moment scholars are again devoting their attention to the investigation of facts: the younger Clark starts again with an exact investigation of the most minute relationships of real economic life, as it appears in present-day questions of economics and sociology, and from here arrives, by means of gradual induction, at the knowledge of more general truths. . . . (pp. 327–28)

What, then, should be the core of the scientific method in economics? Clark's answer is: in "taking account of all relevant facts and excluding none." The emphasis on *relevant* facts is important to Clark, and it is also a striking anticipation of the concern for relevance in the 1960s and early 1970s.

Clark, in his own era, obviously felt sympathetic to that question when he observed that in the future, economic students might rightly insist that their study be focused around the major problems of their own time and place. They would also crave, he prophesied, some orienting framework of ideas that can give coherence to the whole picture, provided this framework were relevant.

Indeed, Clark found the scientific search for relevance of both fact and theory to be the answer to a question that puzzled many in the 1930s, 1940s, and even 1950s. "What is the source of the great appeal of the 'Keynesian' economics? One obvious answer is that it takes hold of the problem which the interwar experience drove home deep in the feelings of mankind as the major sickness of Western economic society, and it does so with an analysis that commands standing as objectively scientific, centering in a formula of the way in which the economic mechanism operates, the analysis being translatable into statistically observable quantities . . ." (EI, p. 14).

SHOULD MATHEMATICS BE TRANSLATED?

As Jesse W. Markham has explained, it is not surprising that Clark, with his emphasis upon bridging the gap between the models of static theory and the dynamic realities of a market economy, did not employ the usual formal models. Markham concludes that "the complexities of these dynamic realities could not be compressed into conventional geometric or algebraic models." That this was a choice and not a necessity is revealed by his citation of work by Cournot and other mathematical economists, and by the fact that he was a charter member and subsequently a fellow of the Econometric Society.

Clark addressed a plea to his mathematically oriented colleagues for communicability and rapprochement. This plea was not based upon skepticism or disbelief about the potential fruitfulness of their work—of its worth he professed no doubt. He was also unconcerned about the likelihood that the results would not be adequately verified—he was content to rely on specialists to catch the errors of others. He was very concerned, however, that the results be put in a form that makes it possible for any economist with analytical power or empirical grasp to appraise the significance of the findings. In short: "What an economist wants to know is what features of the concepts and assumptions used are responsible for the character of the results, and how much difference it would make to the results if these concepts and assumptions were modified by taking in more of the complexities of reality" (ME, p. 77).

As Richard Ruggles points out in the second AEA *Survey* volume, the wisdom or necessity of thus translating or interpreting mathematics has been argued for some time. The debate in the journals subsided some time ago, but it persists to this day on less formal levels. Although Paul Samuelson maintains that the translation of mathematical economics back into literary economics is unrewarding, others (notably Stigler) concur with Clark. Stigler feels that translation is imperative, in order to reduce preoccupation with mathematics on aesthetic grounds, to diminish any preference for elegant solutions of small problems at the expense of intractable larger problems, and to place results before the scrutiny of the whole body of peers. In fairness to the opposing view, and in anticipation of the way the debate seems to have been resolved, Pigou's words, found in his 1952 *Essays in Economics*, should be added to the scales:

To wrap up arguments which are essentially mathematical in such a way as to conceal their true character is extremely cumbersome, greatly swelling up the size of books. Moreover, expert readers are put to unnecessary trouble in *unwrapping* the arguments; for it is often difficult to test their validity or even fully to understand them until they have been reduced again to symbolic form. Conversation is fostered and knowledge advanced if Hindus are allowed to talk to one another in Hindustani, instead of being obliged, in the interest of listening Englishmen—who, after all, *need* not listen—to translate their thoughts into another language. Ought not some economists sometime to have the privilege of these Hindus? (p. 117)

PSYCHOLOGY IN ECONOMICS

It is apparent that anyone interpreting the economics of welfare as broadly as does Clark must sooner or later confront the psychological and ethical implications of such a view. In his case, it was sooner. A celebrated two-issue journal article on the psychological aspects and implications of economics appeared in 1918. Clark's ethical concerns were also apparent very early, although his systematic study of ethics in economic life came during the latter part of his career.

Clark's belief that analysis of economic behavior must involve psychology is clearly articulated in the 1918 articles:

The economist may attempt to ignore psychology, but it is a sheer impossibility for him to ignore human nature, for his science is a science of human behavior. Any conception of human nature that he may adopt is a matter of psychology, and any conception of human behavior that he may adopt involves psychological assumptions, whether these be explicit or no. If the economist borrows his conception of man from the psychologist, his constructive work may have some chance of remaining purely economic in character. But if he does not he will not thereby avoid psychology. Rather he will force himself to make his own, and it will be bad psychology. (PSE, p. 96)

It is scarcely necessary to concern ourselves with the details of Clark's psychology, especially since some of these details necessarily reflect dependence upon the psychology of a half-century ago. The essential features of Clark's view of the human condition, however, remain relevant today. The individual is a social as well as an autonomous animal; he is motivated by more than a narrowly conceived self-interest; and he receives guidance, much of which might be improved.

Clark asserted that in their basic physical needs, people are much alike. Thus, the conventional view of economists that we can know nothing about the relative importance of things to different people is the least plausible hypothesis we might accept. Humans are also members of groups and of the larger society, and they are heavily influenced by that membership. Clark contrasts the assumption of much of nineteenth-century economics, (that people have great self-reliance and foresight) with the renewed realization in our century that individuals are molded by their environment. We are also now witnessing massive, deliberate, and self-conscious efforts to control and intensify this molding process.

Human motivation, with its ambivalence between self and others, can scarcely be summed by individual maximization of utility. People identify themselves with others, and with the interests and goals of others. True, self-interest remains a major economic motive. Enlightened self-interest can become a strong constructive force, but if enlightenment merely means taking the long view and treating others as mere means to the end of self, this is contrary to the fundamental ethics of a free and humane society. But the term "enlightened" means more than merely a calculating shrewdness in utilizing others as means. Clark concludes:

. . . Self-interest is not really enlightened unless it is also enlarged until it identifies itself, to some extent at least, with the interests of others. And once this enlargement takes place, it can never treat others as mere means. Enlightenment is an invaluable way of approaching this kind of enlargement, but it is not complete unless the enlargement has taken place. Then what we are doing to others concerns us because it concerns them, and we care what we do to them, wanting it to be constructive. And if "enlightenment" goes this far, it has become ethical. . . . (EI, p. 207)

Clark believed the term that ultimately describes the motivation for action that is best (and also feasible) in a free society is "responsibility," and he concluded that this concept has two sides. First, it describes the attitude of an individual concerning the decisions he makes for himself—an attitude recognizing a margin of discretion and voluntarily exercising that discretion with an eye to the interests of others. Second, the term suggests accountability to others and to the world outside. This need not mean formal legal requirements; it could mean those more general requirements levied by "a decent respect for the opinions of mankind."

People need guidance, and they have always received it in one form or another. Their guidance has come from the amount of information available through such institutions as selling and advertising and from society acting through government. The assumption of total self-guidance that permeated much of nineteenth-century economics was perhaps a convenient fiction. If the individual is his own best guide and judge, or if society is helpless in applying guidance because it cannot penetrate the autonomy of the individual and hence does not know in which direction to guide, then economics can be both noncommital and safe from obvious error. If the individual is not necessarily the best and only judge, or if he is not so unique and isolated from the group as traditional theory assumed, then guidance from society may be in order and economics might wisely develop a theory of guidance.

Clark, in pursuing the latter path, writes: "no judgment of efficiency can be regarded as absolute which arbitrarily closes any door of choice which is in fact open to the will of humanity. To the individual many doors are closed which open to the collective power of society, and this is the fundamental reason why 'social efficiency' means something radically different from the sum of individual efficiencies" (PSE, p. 141).

For example, in a state without effective public employment agencies, each one of a million citizens might reach the maximum efficiency open to him under these circumstances, which no one person as an individual can change. But the million people are not working at the efficiency possible to them collectively if public employment agencies, which would materially reduce the volume of unemployment, could be established.

ETHICS IN ECONOMICS

The casual reader of Clark may be misled or put off by the little moral homilies or exhortations for mutual aid or a better life that he often attached to some quite precise and hardnosed technical analysis. True, Clark did have values he unashamedly set forth—including balance, responsibility, peace, justice, and opportunity. But these were not simply peripheral adjuncts or addenda to this work as an economist. He believed that ethics has a role to play in the most technical of economics, whether that role be recognized, ignored, or simply not perceived.

Clark saw two worlds: one of impersonal analysis of cause and effect; the other a world of desires, ideals, and value judgments. The sciences deal with the first, ethics deals with the second, and economics is called upon to bridge this gap. "It is a science—or tries to be—and its subject matter consists of desires and values."

Economics has several essential links with ethics:

> First, as science, it has one dominant ethical imperative: the imperative to find in accordance with the evidence. Second, the economic life which it studies is built upon a basic ethical requirement: the ethics of voluntary co-operation. Any economic system rests on law and law rests on acceptance. In our kind of system, which economizes coercion, there is all the more need of voluntary acceptance of the ethical standards necessary to co-operation, going beyond what law can possibly embody in its formal requirements. (EI, pp. 31–32)

If economics abdicates its interest in ethics, it becomes potentially dangerous and even antisocial: neutral about ends, preoccupied with means—in short, "power without defined purpose." Further, "It is all the more dangerous because its main instrument—the market—is not a passive instrument but a social institution that acts as if it had a life and purpose of its own, independent of those of the people who operate it and doing things to them that none of them planned or desired" (EI, p. 33). It will be our ethical and economic master unless we work consciously to achieve whatever of our ends the market fails to fulfill.

But does this make the economist a moralist without license? A lay evangelist rather than a scientist? Clark thought not. His position was a simple one: if an economist wishes to express an ethical judgment, or to make explicit an ethical premise, he will meet his responsibilities as a scientist if he clearly defines the standard he is using and gives enough of the facts to make clear the kind of judgment that necessarily follows. Then the reader or the student, forewarned, can accept or reject his conclusion as they accept or repudiate his standard.

CLARK AS EXEMPLAR

J. M. Clark wrote a great deal about how economists should ply their trade. He also provided a living example, extended over more than five decades and revealed in a vast output of published works and through teaching and public service. It may well be that the example spoke even more loudly than the words, although neither contradicted the other.

In retrospect, one of the striking aspects of Clark's approach to his discipline was his constant determination to relate theory and reality, never abandoning one for the pursuit of the other. He was, from the very beginning, a theorist—not only in the conventional macro and micro fields, but in virtually every subject he touched. Description per se never interested him very much.

Yet, he was enormously knowledgeable about the American economy, about our larger society, about economic history and the history of thought—about all manner of things. In company with Smith, Marshall, Pigou, and others whom he admired, he had an itch to know. He did not, unlike Wesley Mitchell, contribute very much through the accumulation of original data. He had great skill, however, in utilizing such data, in making discriminations, in interpretation, and, above all, in putting it in such juxtaposition with theory that facts and ideas were mutually illuminated. The phrase "descriptive analysis" fits his approach very neatly.

Clark also displayed in his writings, including some continuing professional dialogues with differing peers, a reasonableness, openness, and objectivity that disarmed where it did not always persuade. As noted by Galbraith, in his review (see Bibliography) of *Economic Institutions and Human Welfare,* Clark has dealt in half a century of teaching and writing with virtually all of the most troubling and controversial issues of social policy. But, Galbraith concludes, "More than any other economist of his generation, John Maurice Clark has transcended controversy. . . . his conclusions have been cased in a framework of patient and meticulous and reasonable argument which not only dissipates hostility but goes far to preclude argument" (p. 3).

Kenneth Boulding, in reviewing (see Bibliography) the same book, notes how difficult it is to review a book by which one is deeply moved. He sums up his reaction:

> There is so much ripe wisdom here, such beautifully balanced judgment, with a warm, hopeful concern for the deeper aspects of human welfare balanced by a sharp analytical realism, that one is content simply to enjoy, to savor, and to consent. Throughout these essays runs a plea for a balanced, pragmatic approach to economic institutions, for what the author calls "constructive serviceability." Let us have private enterprise where that is most effective, public enterprise where *that* is most effective, governmental and legal frameworks to prevent unreasonable fluctuations or intolerable inequities and let us always remember that the fundamental object of the economic system is not the production of commodities, which are all merely intermediate goods, but of rich and interesting human lives. Let us beware of ideologies, whether of rigid *laissez-faire* or of doctrinaire socialism; let us treasure the freedom of the individual, but not be afraid to limit it by law in the interest of greater freedom for all, and let us inculcate the habit of responsible behavior, without which freedom inevitably destroys itself. (p. 1004)

Clark brought to his task not only diverse skills, dogged persistence, and wide-ranging knowledge, but also the mixture of scientist and sage, scholar and evangelist, that J. M. Keynes once noted in Alfred Marshall. Indeed, the prescription by Keynes (in his sketch of Marshall, found in *Essays in Biography*) of the requisite qualities of a (great) economist, which he found largely fulfilled by Marshall, seems remarkably apropos of J. M. Clark as well:

> The study of economics does not seem to require any specialised gifts of an unusually high order. Is it not, intellectually regarded, a very easy subject compared with the higher branches of philosophy and pure sci-

ence? Yet good, or even competent, economists are the rarest of birds. An easy subject, at which very few excel! The paradox finds its explanation, perhaps, in that the master-economist must possess a rare *combination* of gifts. He must reach a high standard in several different directions and must combine talents not often found together. He must be mathematician, historian, statesman, philosopher—in some degree. He must understand symbols and speak in words. He must contemplate the particular in terms of the general, and touch abstract and concrete in the same flight of thought. He must study the present in the light of the past for the purposes of the future. No part of man's nature or his institutions must lie entirely outside his regard. He must be purposeful and disinterested in a simultaneous mood; as aloof and incorruptible as an artist, yet sometimes as near the earth as a politician. (pp. 140–41, Norton)

‹ 5 ›

In Retrospect

How, after all this, does one classify, catalogue, and assign to J. M. Clark a neat and proper niche in the ongoing assemblage of economists? What impact has he had upon the continuing development of economics? By now it should be evident that easy, simplistic answers to such questions are hard to come by. Indeed, his career suggests that the questions may be simplistic too. He saw a complex world, with many grays and many footnotes, and perhaps we owe him a comparable appraisal.

Clark has even frustrated those who would assign him to a "school" or an established approach. Was he a neoclassicist, an institutionalist, a pre-Keynesian, a welfare economist, a political economist, or some other identifiable kind of economist? His professional interests also covered such a vast range, as this essay suggests only in small part (and the bibliography scarcely better), that he cannot easily be consigned to a compartment as a price theorist, a student of business cycles, or as any other kind of topical specialist. In truth, he was all of these things, yet in the sense that he would not let his world have close-in walls, he was none of them.

He represents, in some large part, a "constructive synthesis" between divergent (and to others, clashing) general approaches, focal points, and methods. Jacob Oser refers to him as an institutionalist with roots in neoclassicism, and in a broad sense a welfare economist. Joseph Dorfman entitles a chapter "John Maurice Clark: The Constructive Synthesis of Tradition and the New Dynamics," and recalls that Clark sought, in his own words, a "social-institutional-dynamic economic theory." Dorfman finds in Clark's work an integrated synthesis of neoclassical economics and institutionalism. John McDonald, in a December, 1950 issue of *Fortune*, (see Bibliography) asserts:

Without much acclaim outside the profession, he anticipated most of the modern schools, and then absorbed their later developments. . . . Consequently he has been labeled with the names of nearly all schools but Marxist. . . . he is one of the most vigorous intellects in the profession and the embodiment of that new classical synthesis that has come over the profession, and that came over him some time ago. (p. 110)

Is he, then, simply the creator in life and in writings of a synthesis useful for his era but perhaps soon relegated to history? The question, of course, is itself debatable, in the light of the great usefulness and durability of some of the eclectic benchmarks of economic literature. In any case, this essay has suggested that although he did consciously build bridges, and was himself a bridge, he was never merely that. His remembered and built-upon contributions to economic theory; his fastidious and still-interesting studies utilizing his twin passions for accurate description and analysis; his still-relevant strictures about the futility of methodological bickering and the necessity of pursuing problems wherever they may lead and using any relevant method in that pursuit; and his prophetic insights concerning labor as an overhead cost, the nature of social costs and social values, and his social approach to interpersonal comparisons—all of these make Clark more than a consignee to history-of-thought texts.

A final question, nominally about Clark but perhaps actually about economics, needs to be asked. Would he be an anachronism today? Can there be other men of his sort, and if so, will they rise to his distinction?

Boulding confronts this question, obliquely, in his 1957 review:

There is something peculiarly American in the thought of J. M. Clark: it stems from the sweet reasonableness of Penn and of Emerson, from the pragmatism of William James, from what might be called the Gentle Tradition in American life. It stands over against the harshness and cruelty both of Manchester and of Marx, with their confident solutions and roughshod ideologies. To some extent too it stands over against the bright young world of the econometricians and operations researchers, though this is not brought out in these essays. There is always a danger of course that the gentle may degenerate into the genteel without some stiffening from the tough-minded, and some critics might feel that Clark's thought is a little too "tender"—that it does not wrestle enough with the difficult quantitative questions of how much and just when! Nevertheless in an age that is too tough, too cruel, and too brittle, long on knowledge and short on wisdom, there is an important place for a gentle, kindly, and wise approach to the problem of the economic ideal. (pp. 1004–05)

Dewey, in summing his review of Clark's last book, seems somewhat less sanguine:

The education that J. M. Clark received belongs to another age, at any rate on this side of the Atlantic. It is not merely that he had our first great economist as friend and teacher. The specialized programs of the American graduate school and fragmented course offerings of its college are not calculated to produce the unique combination of qualities that distinguished the work of the Clarks—a sure grasp of economic theory, a sense of history, an unashamed commitment to doing good, and a self-confidence that directed their energies to important subjects. There is even the danger that a badly educated, even though well trained, younger generation will not fully appreciate the achievement of an economist who, after examining an intricate problem in theory, can accept that he "is for the most part reduced to speaking of what is likely or unlikely, rather than of what is bound to happen." (pp. 88–89)

He adds: "Let us hope not." One can only echo that hope.

J. M. Clark
and His Peers:
A Postscript

During his career J. M. Clark wrote scores of book reviews, biographical sketches, and memorial essays. From these materials may be drawn an absorbing glimpse of Clark's views about the work of his distinguished peers. Perhaps in the process we may also gain a final insight into Clark's own work, which presumably serves as a frame of reference for his appraisal of others. *J. M. Clark and His Peers*, which follows, is intended to serve both of these ends.

Although a few of these critiques were written retrospectively, in mid- or late-career, most of them have the immediacy, insight, hedging, and occasional error that mark estimates made "with the ballots not yet in" and with the historians of economic thought not yet granted custody. To assist the reader, the dates of Clark's evaluations are given.

The peers were not selected at random, yet others could have been chosen. There is no special significance in ordering or in length, except that the latter and longer excerpts—about Veblen, Mitchell, Hobson, Cooley, and especially his father—focus upon men who had a special impact upon J. M. Clark, as mentors or as supportive contemporaries or both.

Some of Clark's estimates of the work of his contemporaries are but fragments; they focus on the ideas and never on the man; and a generosity of spirit pervades nearly all of them. Clark's appraisals were incisive and often critical, but they were never petty nor mean. As Pigou remarked in *Economics in Practice*, with reference to the criticism often leveled at Marshall for being overgenerous in his interpretation of the thought of others, if this be a fault, "it is a great man's fault, not a little man's."

ON ALFRED MARSHALL (1921)

This volume [*Industry and Trade*] appeared under circumstances which may amount to something of a handicap. It has been awaited and looked forward to so much that it would be only natural if unreasonable expectations had been formed of it. It was to have contained the conclusion of Professor Marshall's thinking. And Marshall's mind is so many sided as to appeal to many economists of different types. Each has probably found in his writing fragments indicating an unusually long reach or keen insight into just those ranges of principle or areas of phenomena in which he, the reader, saw the key to the most fruitful developments. In the new volume, then, each may expect to find those germs which he himself had most cherished, developed, and brought to fruition as an economic system. One is tempted to expect a theory of social economics more real than anything that has hitherto appeared because of the large awareness of such things which one finds (often in footnotes) in the "Principles." One is even tempted to expect that at last the true and proper *liaison* will be established between abstract theory and concrete realism. In all these respects, however, anything approaching finality is quite too much to expect, and it is equally unreasonable to expect Marshall to satisfy all the conflicting groups which find something in his thought to borrow from, and would like to find more. . . .

ON A. C. PIGOU (1913)

There is a current play in which the heroine says to the hero, who has just avowed his devotion in distinctly unusual terms: "How dare you tell me such an interesting thing in such a horrid way?" Professor Pigou's book (*Wealth and Welfare*) has already gained well-deserved praise from Professor Edgeworth, and there is little danger that its brilliant quality and significance will go unappreciated among students of economics, who should be sufficiently hardened to withstand the somewhat benumbing effect of its style. So that if the present writer seems overcritical, Professor Pigou will understand that the very merits of the work make one resent its faults the more.

The book is a general treatise with a special point of view and method of attack which put the author's personal mark on everything he touches, from index numbers to outdoor relief. The point of view is the constant inquiry how society can get the maximum satisfaction-income from economic goods and services, and the method is an unusually keen and exacting deductive analysis, fortified with citations of fact which show remarkably wide and varied knowledge. But the *a priori* reasoning ever takes first place. Indeed, the author, in discussing the relative efficiency of public and private operation of utilities, frankly throws statistics out of court, as being vitiated by the disturbing factors of each individual case, and prefers to rely on the *a priori* balancing of two forces making for efficiency and four others making against it. Fortunately, the result with which he emerges is such as to corroborate the conclusions of the statisticians. . . .

ON J. M. KEYNES (1948)

And while history is making up its ponderously changeable mind, the best hints it can give us may come from a comparison with Keynes's great antithesis, Ricardo.

Indeed, the similarities in the work of the two men are surprising: in their methods, their strong points, and their defects. Each formulated brilliant deductive theories, growing out of contemporary events, conditions, and issues, as only the greatest deductive structures do. Both structures were left incomplete, with shortcomings of organization and terminology; and both men would have done some revising had they lived, either in the text or by separate commentary. And each left a school of disciples, many of them more orthodox than the master, lending the support of their doctrines to a one-sided emphasis in policy, which in Ricardo's case has been only gradually worn away by a century of erosion. . . .

From one standpoint, Keynes merely rediscovered things practical men knew before Adam Smith; and developed implications that make most practical men distrust the whole structure. But for conventional economics the effect of the Keynesian propositions is startling. Its one world seems to be split into two realms of logic, and the sense of one is the nonsense of the other. When relativity upset Newtonian physics, we were at least told that it would not make any perceptible difference to the man driving a car or operating a lathe. But these economic ideas come into the realm of everyday policy and give us opposite prescriptions for matters such as wages or balancing the budget. It is a good deal as if the world we have to work in were on both sides of Alice's looking-glass at once, so that we never know, when we see a garden and want to get into it, whether the thing to do is to walk toward it or away from it. Alice at least knew on which side of the looking-glass she was at any one time. . . .

How is one to tell which kind of law applies in a given case: laws from the orthodox front side or the Keynesian back side of the looking-glass? The simplest formula is that Keynesian laws apply until we get full employment, and orthodox laws after that. This is a rough guide. . . . Another hypothesis is that Keynesian laws apply to short-run movements and orthodox laws to long-run equilibria; but this hardly fits the case. . . .

And so there seems to be no machine-made way of deciding which kind of law holds. Neither tells us all about a given case, and the only thing to do is to examine each problem in the light of the possibilities suggested by both kinds of theory. If and when one arrives at an answer, it will probably be found to go beyond the simple formulas of either kind. The Keynesian formula is a striking antithesis to orthodoxy, where just such a striking antithesis was needed to break through the crust of outworn ideas. It remains for the next generation to fashion a synthesis, both in theory and in policy.

ON J. R. HICKS (1940)

This [*Value and Capital*] is a serious work for hardened students of advanced economic theory. In it the author —now Stanley Jevons Professor at the University of Manchester—has the boldness to undertake to formulate a unified and systematic structure of pure economic theory which deals with the field of dynamics as well as with statics, and ends by laying the groundwork for an interpretation of business fluctuations. The sustained analytical power displayed must command the highest respect. The work has the aspect of a single long chain of deduction, with guy-ropes at fairly frequent intervals in the shape of consideration of the verisimilitude of particular assumptions. (However, the author often appears satisfied if an assumption bears a moderate resemblance to some of the main features of reality.) One end of the chain is anchored to the foundations of static equilibrium; the other seems at times to be swinging loose in a gusty area where "anything can happen." . . .

. . . The present reviewer's expectation is that the author's whole system will not find complete acceptance, but that some of his particular tools of analysis will approve themselves by use, and will make their way—possibly with modifications—into general currency.

The author adopts the device of indifference curves as a substitute for the traditional marginal-utility analysis, in the attempt to avoid doubtful psychological assumptions. Yet it appears that the principal psychological assumption—that of a scale of preferences with sufficient stability to express itself in an organized and consistent budget—remains. And the concept of total utility also appears: a concept which seems more doubtful psychologically than that of marginal comparisons. . . .

The book contains an unusually large number of propositions, presented with great conciseness. In fact, appraisal would have been easier if the material had been more fully developed. Professor Hicks has given us plenty to think about, and it deserves to be thought about with the greatest seriousness, even if quick and definitive appraisals may not be forthcoming.

ON WERNER SOMBART (1931)

In any case, the reader [of *Die Drei Nationalökonomien*] is left in no doubt as to what Sombart stands for and what he opposes. Pure theory deals with fictions, and the fictions he prefers are of a bolder sort than the Austrian speculations. He speaks for the analysis of economic society into its necessary elements, the determination of all possible species of such elements, and the recombining of them into all possible (humanly compatible) combinations. The whole process results in nothing less than an array of all logically possible economic systems. Whether these are found historically in pure form does not matter; but their use is to give an understanding of the rationale of actual historical systems. . . .

. . . If Sombart's interest had been less occupied with the broad perspectives of change in institutions and in dominant ideas, and more with the specific operations of parts of a given economic system, the emphasis might well have been different; tho that is no matter for regret. Perhaps the main thing is that he has spoken boldly for the scientific validity of theoretical methods adapted to grappling with living historical realities. Rejecting the older system-theories, he remains a theorist. . . .

ON GUSTAV CASSEL (1924)

An occasional impression of academic unreality is largely accounted for by the fact that the author is undertaking [in *A Theory of Social Economy*] to discover universal laws representing those features of our existing system which are independent of human institutions. The result is the hypothetical building-up of a system based on the bare assumptions of need, scarcity, free choice on the part of individuals between possible gratifications and the search on the part of the community for the most efficient possible utilization of its limited resources. These premises are taken to carry with them the system of free exchange at uniform prices. The main outlines of the resulting system are of the type called "orthodox" in America, though the author specifically rejects marginal utility, cost and marginal productivity as causes of values or distributive shares; on the ground that they are not ultimate independent variables, but are themselves determined by the true independent forces in the case. Most "orthodox" theorists would probably agree with everything Cassel says on this point, except for the conclusion that these particular concepts are totally useless. . . .

His form of explanation of the forces governing value and distribution ignores psychology, all but ignores differences in buying power, and centers in a series of equations, expressing in symbolic form the fact that the demand-schedule for every commodity is a function of the prices of *all* the other commodities. . . .

ON FRIEDRICH A. HAYEK (1949)

Hayek's position on economic policy is baffling: stressing the function of the free market and the dangers of expanding public controls, admitting the necessity of a considerable measure of control, but avoiding adequate definition of the line between the controls he opposes and those he would approve. The present volume [*Individualism and Economic Order*] contributes little to clarification of this vagueness. This is partly because the volume is a collection of short essays and addresses, in which Hayek repeatedly excuses himself from systematic and specific elaboration on grounds of lack of space; but it seems to be more fundamentally a matter of Hayek's method of attacking the analysis of these problems.

He starts with a principle, which he emphasizes as of dominant importance. He then admits that an opposing principle has validity and some proper scope; but never comes to grips with the question how far the opposing principle may properly be carried, and how it may be kept down to sound methods and limits. This is a fairly common theoretical method of analysis; and amounts to throwing the pragmatic emphasis, which generally accompanies the inevitable oversimplification of theory, in one direction or the other. If this direction is that in which the next steps need to be taken, this pragmatic effect may be useful, so far as it goes and so long as only those next steps are in consideration. If the emphasis is thrown in the opposite direction, as Hayek's is, its usefulness is limited to sounding a very general warning against possible excesses or wrong methods, but without yielding much useful guidance to those who are earnestly seeking it, aware of dangers but aware also of things that must be done. . . .

In general, Hayek seems to underrate amazingly the seriousness of the problem of assured employment, and the extent of the public intervention it makes inevitable. He pitches his argument on a mechanistic economic level, and seems simply intolerant of attitudes that do not fit such a scheme, rather than recognizing their existence and seeking a viable adjustment with them. On this basis, he seems doomed to the role of Cassandra.

ON THORSTEIN VEBLEN (1929, 1959)

As to the merits of his work, opinions differ more widely and more fervently than on any other writer of equal prominence. He is rated among the great economists of history, or as no economist at all; as a great original pioneer or as a critic and satirist without constructive talent or achievement. And he was, one might almost say, all of these things; from different standpoints and by different criteria, each of which it is possible to understand and even to appreciate. One thing at least can be said. If he chose to paint after a futurist technique of his own devising, it was not for lack of capacity to master the academic canons. He had thought them through to his own satisfaction and passed on to other areas of inquiry which appeared to him more interesting and more fruitful.

His critical essays probably left the majority of readers, who were not forewarned and prepared, resentfully rubbing numerous sore spots and wondering with some bewilderment what it was all about. They were criticised for not doing what they had never set out to do, and for not being what it had never occurred to them to be; while the worth of what they had undertaken was brushed aside with airy disparagement. And Veblen's style resembled a barbed-wire entanglement, difficult to penetrate and with rapier-sharp points to prick the unwary. Those who quickly dismissed the problem are probably those who have not seen Veblen as an economist at all, or have seen him as merely a critic and satirist. Those who continued to wonder, and to some purpose, owe him

the greatest of educational experiences: that of being forced to
rethink their basic conceptions, and to make terms of some sort
with a radically different point of view which could not be wholly
dismissed. . . .

Veblen's analysis, then, is not the completely objective tracing
of impersonal sequences of cause and effect which his essays on
method call for; but is—as anything human must probably be—a
matter of selected aspects. One of the unanswered puzzles about
this intriguing thinker, at least to those who did not know him
intimately, is his own attitude toward this subjective element
entering into his avowedly objective treatment. It may be a trait
of genius to combine clear consciousness of method with a gift of
leaping over some of the steps and intuitively seizing tools apt to
the securing of desired effects. . . .

Doubtless the facts did dictate the interpretation Veblen gave
them—he being what he was. But among the most controlling of
these facts was the selective emphasis he found in the orthodox
treatment. And by presenting selected aspects calculated to offset
those of orthodoxy, he has rendered the greatest possible service
toward a better balanced treatment than either. And in this matter balance is probably the closest approach to objectivity of
which the human mind is capable. This end, needless to say,
cannot be attained by blind discipleship, but by a discriminating
assimilation. . . .

Was Veblen an economist? He was not a mere economist,
certainly. A philosopher first, and then a student of human cul-
tures, he was always interested in these things for their own sakes
as well as in their relation to purely economic facts. Was he a
scientist? He was not, perhaps, by the criterion of John Stuart
Mill, who held that it was only by virtue of competition and
competitive equilibria that economists can be scientists at all. But
that criterion can no longer be said to be orthodox.

Was Veblen "constructive"? Not in the sense of constructing a
"system" of defined levels of equilibrium or other definitive results. . . . Not in the sense of making his work an outgrowth of
previous orthodoxy. . . . Not in the sense of furnishing his
followers a complete substitute for that orthodoxy in the form of
propositions with which to solve all problems. . . . But if an
independent explanation of important and neglected ranges of
economic facts be constructive, Veblen meets the mark in gener-
ous measure. . . .

ON WESLEY C. MITCHELL (1931)

Homan's suggestion that Mitchell's method of work has colored his conclusions can hardly be other than true, but it does not follow that the basic character of his views is a mere rationalization of the bent of statistical workmanship.

The pyrotechnics of Veblen's battle with the orthodox left Mitchell not simply dazzled and confused, but grappling with the stubborn question: How important were the factors which Veblen emphasized and orthodox theory circumnavigated, compared to those which orthodox theory emphasized and Veblen slighted? A question of quantitative potentialities! One may conjecture that Mitchell's natural leanings received aid and comfort from Veblen's doctrine of replacing assumed harmonies by an observed sequence of matter-of-fact cause and effect. For, while Veblen preached this doctrine, Mitchell practices it—as nearly as may be and with reservations as to the meaning attached to "cause and effect" which will appear later.

It is quite natural that Mitchell refuses to subordinate quantitative economics to the function of verifying the conclusions of traditional deductive theory, or to be worried by the fact that, as yet, quantitative economics has not gotten far with this task. In his view, traditional theory suggests problems and hypotheses, but they are likely to be recast in the process of adapting them to the test of observed behavior; while observation will itself suggest other problems whose standing is in no way inferior merely because traditional "theory" may ignore them. . . .

The most obvious difference between this method and that of traditional theory is that Mitchell reasons from conduct to conditioning motive and circumstance, while traditional theory, in appearance at least, reasons from motive and circumstances to "normal" conduct. Mitchell insists that he would not trust himself to use his analysis of motive and circumstance as a basis for predicting conduct without constant check by observations of actual behavior. Theory, being interested in "normal" behavior, has no such hesitation; variations of behavior from normal are merely the results of other than normal causes. The normal behavior of equilibrium theory is highly simplified and differs from actual behavior. But is not Mitchell simplifying also, to a less extent, in picturing the normal cycle and giving separate recognition to variations from it? At certain points in his analytic description he notes alternative versions of behavior, while every cycle has some features which are unique. His picture of determining conditions is comprehensive, including many of the "disturbing factors" of traditional theory. It is also too complex to permit the mind to deduce a result which is uniquely determined and exact. And it is the lack of this quality, in all probability, which causes some readers to miss the feeling of definite explanation which they get from more traditional methods. . . .

An assimilation of Mitchell's results should certainly challenge the most orthodox theorist to produce some modifications in the traditional analysis, other than a slight lengthening of the chapter on business cycles in that part of the theorist's treatise labeled "special problems" or "applied economics." Shall we ever see the general economic theory which would be the logical outcome of an approach to the whole subject via Mitchell's study of cycles? Or will the effects of Mitchell's study be merged with the results of growing knowledge in many other realms of economic phenomena and motives?

ON J. A. HOBSON (1940)

Fifty-one years ago a book appeared in England, entitled *The Physiology of Industry*, under the joint authorship of a business man of varied interests named Mummery, and an economist, not yet thirty, named John A. Hobson. In this book the authors dared to espouse and develop the thesis that over-saving and underspending could and did exist, and constituted a disease of the industrial system, and a cause of recurrent periods of depression and unemployment. To the academic economists of the period, this doctrine was an utter and outrageous fallacy, disproved by one of the fundamental axioms of their science. Extended and specific refutation appeared hardly necessary, and was not forthcoming. The young economist was promptly labeled "unsound," and passed into outer darkness, so far as the regular economic fraternity were concerned: an exile for which some later connections with the London School of Economics only partly compensated.

Today the central idea of Hobson's original heresy has been adopted, in altered form and with a shifted emphasis, by economists of unquestioned standing, and around it centers what is perhaps the most active and potent body of frontier thinking. Serious investigation of this former heresy has become unqualifiedly respectable. It is true that Hobson's views differed, especially in later formulations, from the present theories, which emphasize underinvestment relative to savings. Hobson concentrated on excessive investment relative to demand, this being socially unprofitable and unprofitable to business as a whole, and tending to destroy the value of previously-existing investments in ways which were socially parasitic. Yet this feature is not to be rejected merely because the present emphasis lies elsewhere. As a step in the process leading to a falling-off in investment it may deserve a place in a balanced synthesis.

It did not fit in with orthodox conceptions of the nature of markets and of normal competition, and even a neo-Marshallian interventionist like Pigou took occasion briefly to dispose of it by showing that the destruction of values was offset by gains passed on to consumers, and was not really parasitic. Yet this refutation rested on a conception of perfect markets and perfect competition which Hobson—rightly as it seems today—denied. On this point a thoroughgoing argument between the two men might have led to an adjustment not wholly unfavorable to Hobson.

This is perhaps typical of the incomplete joining of issues between Hobson and the regular economics. Hobson felt that his views had been ignored rather than refuted; and he in turn never buttressed them by meeting, step by step, all the items in the thoughtful academician's reaction—the alternate ways of "taking account" of the factors urged by Hobson or of justifying rejection of them. Orthodoxy usually has a reasoned justification of its position which it does not feel called upon to mobilize afresh in response to every attack, and this leads the attacker to feel that his views have been unreasoningly rejected. If there is fault in all this, it is probably mutual. Both appear partly right, both partly wrong. And the amazingly prolific semijournalistic writing into which Hobson was impelled was not a favorable instrument for bridging this gap.

The *Evolution of Modern Capitalism* partly restored Hobson's credit in academic quarters. It was a solid study; and while it contained in germ form most of the author's disturbing ideas, they were mostly not generalized as laws and labeled as attacks on accepted theory. To this extent they could be regarded as history—and disregarded as far as the corpus of theory was concerned. Orthodoxy will tolerate presentation of the most devastating evils as history, where it will rise in wrath if a fraction of these evils are presented as laws of the economic order in contradiction to accepted theory. It is not too much disturbed by the idea of evolution so long as it can manage to regard evolutionary change as confined to the content of the life to which its theory applies, while the theory itself can remain formal, and indifferent to changes in the content which is poured into it.

To Hobson, of course, such a defense mechanism was wholly insufficient. And today, apart from questions as to the correctness of his specific propositions, it appears that on this underlying issue he was essentially right. Changing conditions are compelling changes in the structure of theory of the type that analyzes the operation of given conditions, as well as challenging us with the more baffling and elusive urge toward theories of change itself. . . .

Lastly, we come to a theme which was first as well as last in Hobson's thinking: namely, his development of Ruskin's thesis: "There is no wealth but life." This development appears in his *Work and Wealth* and later, with altered emphasis, in *Wealth and Life*. Here the imperfect and biased character of the market as a vehicle for registering actual individual preferences is combined with an insistence on taking account of the imperfections of these preferences themselves as indices of human values, and on this foundation is built an attempt to revalue the standards of the market in terms of an independent criterion of "organic social welfare."

With the recognition that utility is not, as Bentham taught, a homogeneous quantity, but a matter of qualitative differences, economics loses its supposed character of a quantitative science of human values as measured in monetary prices. It must become qualitative, and the judgment of the disinterested public expert has a growing place as against the valuations of the market. The organic character of welfare includes a recognition that the individual is essentially a member of a group, though obviously not the totalitarian abuses of this principle. It also maintains that individual welfare is an organic whole, not to be understood in terms of marginal increments of specific goods and services, any more than a painting is to be understood in terms of the separate values of particular brush strokes. While this principle does not justify an ignoring of marginal units, it seems to deserve more active development than it is likely to get from the theoretical economist's treatment of "complementary utilities." One supremely important value the market neglects is that inhering in the quality of productive effort, which may in itself be positive or negative, largely according as effort is creative or routine. . . .

These brief remarks may give some indication of Hobson's strength and limitations: his lack of definitive formulation and of a completely integrated system, and the vital importance of the truths he laid hold on and the significances he did develop. It is these last which have earned him high rank in the "brave army of heretics"—a heretic undiscouraged and, so far as a mere reader can judge, unembittered.

ON CHARLES HORTON COOLEY (1919)

One wonders if Professor Cooley's reputation for profundity ever suffers because one always knows what he is talking about, and it always means something that has to do definitely with the affairs and interests of real people. . . . [Sociology] "cannot avoid being difficult, but it should be as little abstruse as possible. If it is not human it is nothing." Need one add that he has earned the right to advocate this standard?

Yet he is not afraid of abstractions. At the start he introduces his reader to the idea that such things as languages, myths, and styles of architecture are impersonal forms of life, having tendencies, waging conflicts, growing and decaying without the conscious connivance or recognition of the particular persons through whom their life-processes are carried on.

It is obviously impossible to summarize a book which covers the whole range of current life and presents the ripe judgments of a mind of unusual scope, penetration, and flexibility. He finds that society is not merely an organism but many organisms. He prefers to call them organisms rather than organizations, because organization suggests a tool fashioned to a conscious purpose, whereas these forms of social life grow by the tentative process of trial and selection. In this process the designed policies of men are but experiments. If they work, they grow and change in growing; if they do not work, they are discarded. These phases of life are endlessly interrelated, baffling any attempt to study the world in compartments and causing every special study to ramify until it embraces the whole universe. This creates an illusion like the illusion of the rows of trees in an orchard, which obligingly choose whatever point the observer is standing as the point from which to radiate. They do truly radiate from that point—also from every other. The economic interpretation of history and other forms of particularism—dare one suggest also the central place of the theory of value and distribution in economic thought?—are examples of this combination of truth and error. Social change, being a tentative, organic growth, cannot be predicted in mechanical fashion, but it may to some slight extent be foreseen through an effort of creative imagination by a mind which has entered into the spirit of the life with which it deals. . . .

For the economist, aside from the fact that it is good for him to see the world as a whole, the book contains much of an economic character, and it is equally good to see what economic facts and ideas look like to one who has formed the habit of viewing the world as a whole. Professor Cooley is closer to the economist than most of his fellow-sociologists, and his reactions on economic matters are entitled to corresponding weight. He finds that the Industrial Revolution, like any great and sudden unforeseen change, produced a demoralization in the social mind from which we have only partly emerged. He finds that economic opportunity must be made a social science, since it "calls for a knowledge and preparation far beyond what can be expected of unaided intelligence." He condemns the economics that overemphasizes the self-seeking motives, and holds that it requires no unusual virtue to practice emulation in service; granted a group spirit and organization of which such emulation is a part, it needs only the ordinary traits of loyalty and suggestibility. He emphasizes the need of reasonable security for a healthy morale.

The chief interest of the economist, however, will center in the chapters on valuation. . . . Price is an estimate of economic worth made by society. But since society is not one but many organisms, price is the resultant of many estimates of worth by different individuals and classes, formed under the influence of class prestige, tradition, fashion, and other forms of social and economic suggestion, expressed through legal and social institutions which determine the extent to which an estimate of worth is translated into an effective demand, and weighted according to the purchasing power which the various groups can command

—itself a product of social, legal, and economic institutions and of the whole process of production, valuation, and exchange that has gone before. The effect of this view is to dethrone price as an ultimate measure of worth and an ultimate guide of economic efforts, while increasing one's respect for it as an expression of the many sides and many forces of a growing and developing social life. . . .

ON J. B. CLARK

John Bates Clark (1847–1938) was the leading creative economic theorist active in America during the period when Alfred Marshall and the great Austrian marginalists were active abroad. He developed a distinctive form of marginal utility —marginal productivity theory, which he presented not as a completed system, but as a first approximation and an approach to further analysis. His major theoretical work was cast in the form of comparative statics: he constructed the model of an imaginary "static state"—one of complete competitive equilibrium —following which he analyzed the general effects of hypothetical dynamic changes, including the "dynamic friction" encountered by adjustments to these changes. His work is permeated by a social-ethical perspective that is not always well integrated with the technical economic analysis. Clark was descended from New England Puritans. In him the original rigorous and doctrinaire features of this heritage had been relaxed and humanized, but a powerful religious and moral conviction remained. . . .

Much of Clark's first book, *The Philosophy of Wealth*, consists of criticism of classical economics, and there is in it no constructive theory so completely worked out as that in his more famous *Distribution of Wealth*. In the earlier book Clark stressed the organic social character of economic processes and values. Although individual choices may be made marginally, they are nevertheless socially conditioned, since market forces are in fact integrated through social judgments embodied in the legal system. Instead of seeing self-centered interest alone as the key to human nature, Clark considered people to be motivated by a rational balance between different kinds of personal interests, self-centered and social.

He criticized classical economics for ignoring the importance of "inappropriable values," for example, those values created when an area is opened by railroads. He distinguished several forms of competition: competition in a framework of prevailing prices he characterized as rivalry in serving, whereas sharp bargaining for favorable departures from the market he classed as a form of plunder. When competition had already passed through both the conservative rivalry phase and the later destructive rivalry phase and had begun to move toward consolidation and monopoly, he looked favorably on a possible evolution based on producers' cooperation but thought it would succeed only under certain conditions.

He believed that workers need the protection of unions and that every man has the right to a living, particularly if socially generated adjustments prevent him from earning one. He deplored the economic "caste system" that prevails among certain Protestant denominations because it vitiates the spirit of fraternity so important to his religious beliefs. The ethical message of *The Philosophy of Wealth* elicited wide acclaim, as well as some criticism.

In Clark's next major work, *The Distribution of Wealth* (1899), he developed much more fully the marginalist theories for which he became known. His theories were published later than those of the great contemporary marginalists, but, so far as can be determined, they were independently arrived at. Clark separated economic theory into statics and dynamics, presenting the statics first, as a first approximation and an approach to the greater complexities of dynamics. A dynamic analysis was his ultimate objective, but his "dynamics" were what we would now call comparative statics. Thus he depicted the forces acting toward equilibrium by means of an elaborate model of an imaginary society from which dynamic change and disturbance were eliminated, permitting the static forces to act in isolation and to bring processes to their "natural" (static) levels. . . .

The contrast between the morally critical tone of *The Philosophy of Wealth* and the analytical emphasis and optimism of Clark's later theoretical works has suggested to many that his ethical views changed. On this difficult question the present writer is persuaded that the observed differences stem partly from a change in Clark's method of theoretical analysis, that is, his use of a model economy, and partly from his adaptation to new events. Enlightening evidence is afforded by his last economic utterance, a published lecture entitled *Social Justice Without Socialism* (1914).

He no longer recommended producers' cooperation, with its merging of groups or classes; it had not fulfilled his optimistic expectations. Instead, he stressed collaboration between existing groups, in a prospective system of democratically disciplined economic activity amounting to a "welfare state." It seems that the author of *The Philosophy of Wealth* was responding to historical developments without changing his basic values. . . .

SOME 1952 REFLECTIONS

So much of his personal history; what of the America which his work reflects? It was the vigorously-expanding American of the post-Civil War period, preoccupied with its own affairs, and able, so far, to shrug off the setbacks of intermittent depressions. It included lusty buccaneering, and ominous signs of monopoly; but these did not seem sufficient to vitiate the drive of creative effort which was clearly there. Clark knew that business men were not all saints, nor were they all pirates. In his experience they were prevailingly honest and constructive. With the background which we have already traced, it was perhaps only natural that, in selecting the most basic elements for the keynotes of his deliberately-simplified picture, he should have sketched a society with grave shortcomings, which could nevertheless be cured or sufficiently alleviated for social health, because it had a core, including a moral core, which was sound. Much depends on whether America can justify that faith, in the face of today's more threatening challenge. The outcome is far from secure, and it was perhaps equally natural that Veblen, with his different background and temperament, should reach a more pessimistic conclusion.

One further point. The setting to which an economist now reacts includes not only the conditions and problems of his time, but the tradition of his discipline, which furnishes him the tools with which he attacks his problems. With this tradition a scholar of Clark's temperament was bound, like his great contemporary Alfred Marshall, to maintain continuity of development, branching out on new courses, but building on what had gone before. We shall see that this is what J. B. Clark did.

Sources

J. M. Clark and his Peers is drawn from these
reviews or essays by J. M. Clark

MARSHALL: Review of *Industry and Trade*. In *Journal of Political Economy*,
29(October 1921):684–89.

PIGOU: Review of *Wealth and Welfare*. In *American Economic Review*,
3(September 1913):623–25.

KEYNES: "Revolution in Economics: After Keynes What?" In *Alternative
to Serfdom*, pp. 91–110 (see Bibliography).

HICKS: Review of *Value and Capital*. In *Political Science Quarterly*,
55(March 1940):127–29.

SOMBART: Review of *Die Drei Nationalökonomien*. In *Quarterly Journal of
Economics*, 45(May 1931):517–21.

CASSEL: Review of *A Theory of Social Economy*. In *Political Science Quarterly*, 39(December 1924):688–90.

HAYEK: Review of *Individualism and Economic Order*. In *Political Science
Quarterly*, 64(March 1949):108–10.

VEBLEN: "Thorstein Bunde Veblen, 1857–1929." *American Economic
Review*, 19(December 1929):742–45.

MITCHELL: "Wesley C. Mitchell's Contribution to the Theory of Business Cycles." In *Methods in Social Science*, pp. 662–80 (see Bibliography).

HOBSON: "John A. Hobson, Heretic and Pioneer (1858–1940)." In *Journal of Social Philosophy*, 5(July 1940):356–59.

COOLEY: Review of *Social Process*. In *Journal of Political Economy*, 27(March 1919):218–21.

J. B. CLARK: "John Bates Clark." In *International Encyclopedia of the Social Sciences*, 2:504–8, David L. Sills, ed. New York: The Macmillan Company and The Free Press, 1968. The concluding two paragraphs are from "J. M. Clark on J. B. Clark." In *The Development of Economic Thought*, pp. 593–612 (see Bibliography).

A Bibliographic Note

This is indeed a partial rather than a complete bibliography, although it does contain a very large and representative sample of Clark's work. It is hoped that it is inclusive enough to provide additional insight into the volume, range, and depth of his half-century of writing, as well as to shed light on both the persistence of his interests and occasional changes in focus or emphasis. In addition, the bibliography is so designed that the reader with only casual interest in Clark can utilize the annotation on the essays and anthologies, while the reader with more intense or specialized interests can use the more detailed listing either to pursue a lead suggested by the essay or to explore Clark's work in those areas left unexplored by the essay. In selecting some of Clark's published work, an equivalent number of items have been left out. Largely although not totally excluded have been fragments, notes, replies, rejoinders, committee reports, testimony, popular pieces, ephemeral items, cold war reactions, pamphlets, book reviews, and journal articles either of lesser import or found in more complete or sophisticated form in some other entry. That final exclusion involves a substantial element of arbitrary judgment and should be regarded as suspect, even though necessary.

In the initial draft of this bibliography, the key journal articles and essays that were reprinted, sometimes with modifications and updating, in Clark's major anthologies were omitted from the journal-article–essay section of the bibliography. This had the unfortunate result of making it difficult to get at these pieces without going through the anthologies, especially if their existence was not already known. Thus, the 1917 acceleration article, probably one of the two most influential articles J. M. Clark ever wrote, was effectively hidden from bibliographic view. The attempted solution to this problem is reflected in the fact that not only are the anthologies broadly annotated, but those journal articles or essays also to be found in the anthologies are marked by an asterisk or a dagger, cueing into the respective anthologies.

The closing section of this partial bibliography includes reaction to Clark's work. Some insightful reviews (some of which are quoted or alluded to in the text) of his books are listed, and a few of the general appraisals of his work are given. No attempt could be made to include even in a more comprehensive bibliography all or even most of the appraisals of specific aspects of Clark's work, although some of these particularized reactions are noted in the text. J. M. Clark worked for more than fifty years over a substantial portion of the landscape of economics, and references to him and expositions or critiques of his work are pervasive in the literature of several subfields of economics. This bibliographic Pandora's Box was left unopened.

The portion of the bibliography listing Clark's writings is arranged in chronological order. This has certain evident advantages in terms of tracing the development and evolution of his work. It also has disadvantages. Alphabetical ordering would be quicker for the reader, but reveals nothing of substance. Topical ordering would be helpful, but so much of Clark's work sprawls over more than one field or fits conventional fields so awkwardly that chronological ordering seemed the best choice.

Bibliography

SELECTED WRITINGS OF J. M. CLARK
(IN CHRONOLOGICAL ORDER)

"Benchmark" books:

1923 *Studies in the Economics of Overhead Costs.* Chicago: University of Chicago Press, pp. xiii, 502. In 13th impression by 1965.

1926 *Social Control of Business.* Chicago: University of Chicago Press, pp. xviii, 483. 2nd ed., New York: McGraw-Hill Book Co., 1939, pp. xvi, 537. Reprinted in 1969 by Augustus M. Kelley, Publishers, New York.

1931 *The Costs of the World War to the American People.* New Haven: Yale University Press, pp. xii, 316. Reprinted in 1970 by Augustus M. Kelley, Publishers, New York, with a new introduction by Joseph Dorfman, "The Relations Among John Maurice Clark, N.A.L.J. Johansen and John Maynard Keynes."

1934 *Strategic Factors in Business Cycles.* New York: National Bureau of Economic Research, pp. xv, 238. Reprinted in 1949 by Augustus M. Kelley, Publishers, New York.

1935 *Economics of Planning Public Works*, National Planning Board, Washington, U.S. Government Printing Office, pp. vi, 194. Reprinted in 1965 by Augustus M. Kelley, Publishers, New York.

1961 *Competition as a Dynamic Process.* Washington: The Brookings Institution, pp. xvii, 501.

Other books of significance:

1910 *Standards of Reasonableness in Local Freight Discrimination* (Ph.D. Thesis, Columbia). New York: Columbia University Press, pp. 157.

1912 (With John Bates Clark). *The Control of Trusts*, Rewritten and enlarged ed., New York: The Macmillan Co., pp. xi, 202. Reprinted in 1971 by Augustus M. Kelley, Publishers, New York, with an introductory essay by Joseph Dorfman, "John Bates and John Maurice Clark on Monopoly and Competition." J. B. Clark published the first edition in 1901.

1937 *The National Recovery Administration* (Report of the President's Committee of Industrial Analysis, J. M. Clark, principal author). House Documents, Vol. 11, 75th Congress, 1st session, Washington, D. C.: U. S. Government Printing Office, pp. xii, 193.

1944 *Demobilization of Wartime Economic Controls.* Committee for Economic Development. New York: McGraw-Hill Book Co., pp. xiii, 219.

1949 *National and International Measures for Full Employment* (with others). Report to the United Nations. Lake Success, New York, pp. 106.

1960 *The Wage-Price Problem.* New York: The American Bankers Association, pp. 68.

Books of essays:

1948 *Alternative to Serfdom* (Five lectures delivered on the William W. Cook Foundation at the University of Michigan, March, 1947). New York: Alfred A. Knopf, pp. xii, 153, vi. 2nd ed. rev., New York: Vintage Books, 1960, pp. 161, vii.
(Wanted: a Balanced Society; The Human Material—Biological Roots and What Grows Out of Them; Competition and Security; Revolution in Economics: After Keynes What?; Toward a Society of Responsible Individuals in Responsible Groups.)

1949 *Guideposts in Time of Change* (Six lectures on the Merrill Foundation at Amherst College, in the winter of 1947–1948). New York: Harper and Brothers, pp. x, 210.
(The Totalitarian Threat; Interpreting the Threat and Meeting It; Objectives Within Our Economy; The Direct Attack: Maintaining High-Level Demand; Sound Structure and Behavior of Prices and Costs; Collective Bargaining and Wages; Changing Balances: Uncommon Requirements for the Common Man.)

Anthologies:

1936 *Preface to Social Economics: Essays on Economic Theory and Social Problems.* New York: Farrar and Rinehart, Inc., pp. xxi, 435. Reprinted in 1967 by Augustus M. Kelley, Publishers, New York.
(This anthology includes a wide-ranging collection of essays and journal articles, nearly all of them previously published, written prior to 1936. Most of Clark's seminal shorter works [to that date] in price theory, business cycle theory, stabilization policy, planning, social economy, welfare economics, statics and dynamics, and the origins, premises, and methods of economics are included.)

1957 *Economic Institutions and Human Welfare*, New York: Alfred A. Knopf, pp. xii, 285, x.
(This anthology includes essays that deal "not with economics in the technical sense, but with some of the human and community factors that underlie it." These essays, most of which had already been published but in several cases are not very accessible, were written largely during the 1940–1955 period, mostly in the latter years. It includes essays on aims of economic life, economic welfare in a free society, the ethical basis of economic freedom, the interpenetration of politics and economics, and free enterprise in a planned economy.)

Encyclopedia essays:

1931 "Diminishing Returns," *Encyclopedia of the Social Sciences.* 15 vols, New York: Macmillan, vol. 5, pp. 144–46.
"Distribution." *Ibid.*, vol. 5, pp. 167–73.

1932 "Government Regulation of Industry." *Ibid.*, vol. 7, pp. 122–29.
"Increasing Returns." *Ibid.*, vol. 7, pp. 639–40.

1933 "Monopoly." *Ibid.*, vol. 10, pp. 623–30.
"Overhead Costs." *Ibid.*, vol. 11, pp. 511–13.

1934 "Statics and Dynamics." *Ibid.*, vol. 14, pp. 352–55.

1968 "Clark, John Bates." In *International Encyclopedia of the Social Sciences*, ed. by David L. Sills, 17 vols. New York: Macmillan and the Free Press, vol. 2, pp. 504–7.

Journal articles, essays and monographs:

(All items also found in reprinted, adapted, or updated form in *Preface to Social Economics* are marked with *; all items similarly found in *Economic Institutions and Human Welfare* are designated by †.)

1911 "Rates for Public Utilities." *American Economic Review*, 1(September):473–87.

1913 "Frontiers of Regulation and What Lies Beyond." *American Economic Review* /s, 3(March):114–25.

1914 "Some Economic Aspects of the New Long and Short Haul

Clause." *Quarterly Journal of Economics*, 28(February):322–37.

*"A Contribution to the Theory of Competitive Price." *Quarterly Journal of Economics*, 28(August):747–71.

"Some Neglected Phases of Rate Regulation." *American Economic Review*, 4(September):565–74.

1915 "The Concept of Value." *Quarterly Journal of Economics*, 29 (August):663–73.

1916 *"The Changing Basis of Economic Responsibility." *Journal of Political Economy*, 24(March):209–29.

1917 *"Business Acceleration and the Law of Demand: A Technical Factor in Economic Cycles," *Journal of Political Economy*, 25 (March):217–35.
(An updating note is added in the *Preface to Social Economy* reprint of this article.)
"The Basis of War-Time Collectivism," *American Economic Review*, 7(December):772–90.

1918 *"Economics and Modern Psychology," Parts I–II. *Journal of Political Economy*, 26(January, February):1–30, 136–66.
"The Theory of National Efficiency in War and Peace." In *Readings in the Economics of War*, ed. by J. M. Clark et al., Chicago: University of Chicago Press, pp. 566–87.

1919 *"Economic Theory in an Era of Social Readjustment." *American Economic Review* /s 9(March):280–90.

1920 "Railroad Valuation as a Working Tool." *Journal of Political Economy*, 28(April):265–306.

1921 *"Soundings in Non-Euclidean Economics." *American Economic Review* /s 11(March):132–47.

1922 "Are We Outgrowing Private Capital?" *World Tomorrow*, 5(December):362–63.
"The Empire of Machines." *Yale Review*, n.s., 12(October):132–43.

1923 "Overhead Costs in Modern Industry." Parts I–III. *Journal of Political Economy*, 31(February, April, and October):47–64, 209–42, 606–31.
(Also to be part of core of *Studies in the Economics of Overhead Costs.*)
"Some Social Aspects of Overhead Costs." *American Economic Review* /s 13(March):50–59.

1924 *"The Socializing of Theoretical Economics." In *The Trend of Economics*, ed. by Rexford G. Tugwell. New York: Alfred A. Knopf, pp. 73–102.

1927 "Adam Smith and the Spirit of '76." In *The Spirit of '76 and Other Essays*. Washington, D.C.: The Robert Brookings Graduate School

of Economics and Government, pp. 61–98. Reprinted in 1966 by
Augustus M. Kelley, Publishers, New York.

"Control of Trade Practices by Competition and Other Forces."
Proceedings of the Academy of Political Science, 12(January):600–7.

"Recent Developments in Economics." In *Recent Developments in the
Social Sciences*, ed. by Edward Cary Hayes. Philadelphia: J. B.
Lippincott Co., pp. 213–306.

"Some Central Problems of Overhead Costs." *Bulletin of the Taylor
Society*, 12(February):287–92.

*"The Relation Between Statics and Dynamics." In *Economic Essays
Contributed in Honor of John Bates Clark*, ed. by Jacob H. Hollander.
New York: The Macmillan Co., pp. 46–70.

1928 *"Adam Smith and the Currents of History." In *Adam Smith
1776–1926*. Chicago: University of Chicago Press, pp. 53–76. Reprinted in 1966 by Augustus M. Kelley, Publishers, New York.

*"Inductive Evidence on Marginal Productivity." *American Economic
Review*, 18(September):449–67.

1929 "Government Control of Industry." *World Tomorrow*, 12(February):74–76.

1931 "The Contribution of Economics to Method in Social Science." In
Essays on Research in the Social Sciences. Washington, D.C.: The
Brookings Institution, pp. 67–85.

"Capital Production and Consumer-Taking." *Journal of Political
Economy*, 39:814–16. A rejoinder by R. Frisch, 40(1932):253–55. A
further word by Clark, 40(1932):691–93. A final word by Frisch,
40:694.

"The War's Aftermath in America." *Current History*, 34(May):
169–74.

*"Wesley C. Mitchell's Contribution to the Theory of Business
Cycles." In *Methods in Social Science*, ed. by Stuart A. Rice. Chicago:
the University of Chicago Press, pp. 662–80.

1932 "Business Cycles: The Problem of Diagnosis." *Journal of the American Statistical Association*, 27(Supplement, March):212–17.

*"Long-Range Planning for the Regularization of Industry." (The
Report of a Subcommittee of the Committee on Unemployment
and Industrial Stabilization of the National Progressive Conference,
J. M. Clark, Ch.). *The New Republic*, 69(January 13):1–23. (Part
Two).

"Roundtable Discussion of Institutional Economics," *American
Economic Review* /s, 22(March):105–16 (Clark's statement pp. 105–6).

1933 "Convulsion in the Price Structure," *Yale Review*, n.s., 22
(March):496–510.

1934 "Factors Making for Instability," *Journal of the American Statistical Association*, 29(Supplement, March):72–74.

*"Productive Capacity and Effective Demand." In *Economic Reconstruction* (Report of the Columbia University Commission). New York: Columbia University Press, pp. 105–26.

1935 *"Cumulative Effects of Changes in Aggregate Spending as Illustrated by Public Works." *American Economic Review.* 25(March): 14–20

1936 *"Past Accomplishments and Present Prospects of American Economics," (Presidential address). *American Economic Review*, 26(March):1–11.

1938 "Basing Point Methods of Price Quoting," *The Canadian Journal of Economics and Political Science*, 4(November):477–89.

John Bates Clark: A Memorial, with A. H. Clark. New York: privately printed, p. 40.

1939 "An Appraisal of the Workability of Compensatory Devices," *American Economic Review /s*, 29(March):194–208.

"Monopolistic Tendencies, Their Character and Consequences." *Proceedings of the Academy of Political Science.* 18(January):124–31.

1940 †"Forms of Economic Liberty and What Makes Them Important." In *Freedom: Its Meaning*, ed. by Ruth Nanda Anshen. New York: Harcourt, Brace.

"The Attack on the Problem of Full Use." In *The Structure of the American Economy, Part II: Toward Full Use of Resources*, National Resources Planning Board. Washington, D.C.: U.S. Government Printing Office, pp. 20–27.

"Toward a Concept of Workable Competition." *American Economic Review*, 30(June):241–56.

1941 "Further Remarks on Defense Financing and Inflation." *The Review of Economic Statistics*, 23(August):107–12.

"Investment in Relation to Business Activity and Employment." In *Studies in Economics and Industrial Relations* by Wesley C. Mitchell et al. University of Pennsylvania Bicentennial Conference, Philadelphia: University of Pennsylvania Press, pp. 37–51.

"The Relation of Government to the Economy of the Future." *Journal of Political Economy*, 49(December):797–816.

1942 "Economic Adjustments After Wars: The Theoretical Issues." *American Economic Review /s*, 32(March):1–12.

How to Check Inflation. Public Affairs Pamphlet No. 64. New York: The Public Affairs Committee, Inc., p. 31.

"Our Economic Freedom," *Annals of the Academy of Political Science*, 220(March):178–85.

"Problems of Price Control." *Proceedings of the Academy of Political Science*, 20(May):11–22.

"Relations of History and Theory." (Symposium on Profits and the Entrepreneur). *Journal of Economic History* /s, 2(December):132–42.

†"The Role of Economics." In *Education for Citizenship Responsibilities*, ed. by Franklin Burdette. Princeton, N.J.: Princeton University Press, pp. 31–38.

1943 "Imperfect Competition Theory and Basing-Point Problems." *American Economic Review*, 33(June):283–300.

"Reply to Professor Clark on Imperfect Competition Theory and Basing-Point Problems," by Vernon A. Mund, and "Rejoinder," by J. M. Clark. *American Economic Review*, 33(September):612–16, 616–19.

1944 "Educational Functions of Economics After the War." *American Economic Review* /s, 34(March):58–67.

"How Not to Reconvert." *Political Science Quarterly*, 59(June):176–92.

"Price Controls in Transition." *Proceedings of the Academy of Political Science*, 21(May):89–99.

1945 "Economic Controls in Postwar Transition." In *Economic Reconstruction*, ed. by Seymour E. Harris. New York: McGraw-Hill, pp. 181–95.

"Financing High-Level Employment." In *Financing American Prosperity: A Symposium of Economists*, Paul T. Homan and Fritz Machlup, eds. New York: The Twentieth Century Fund, pp. 71–125.

"General Aspects of Price Control and Rationing in the Transition Period." *American Economic Review* /s, 35(May):152–62.

1946 "Realism and Relevance in the Theory of Demand." *Journal of Political Economy*, 54(August):347–53.

1947 "Mathematical Economists and Others: A Plea for Communicability." *Econometrica*, 15(April):75–78.

"Some Current Cleavages Among Economists." *American Economic Review* /s, 37(May):1–11.

1949 †"Free Enterprise and a Planned Economy." In *The Christian Demand for Social Justice*, ed. by Bishop William Scarlett. New York: New American Library of World Literature.

"Machlup on the Basing-Point System." *Quarterly Journal of Economics*, 63(August):315–21.

"The Law and Economics of Basing Points: Appraisal and Proposals." *American Economic Review*, 39(March):430–47.

1950 †"Economic Means—To What Ends." In *"The Teaching of Undergraduate Economics"* Supplement in *American Economic Review*, 40, part 2(December):34–51.

"The Orientation of Anti-Trust Policy," *American Economic Review* /s, 40(May):93–104. (Includes 4 pp. of discussion.)

1951 "Criteria of Sound Wage Adjustment, with Emphasis on the Question of Inflationary Effects." In *The Impact of the Union*, ed. by David McCord Wright. New York: Harcourt, Brace, pp. 1–33. Reprinted in 1966 by Augustus M. Kelley, Publishers, New York.

"Policy Recommendations by the Committee on Economic Stabilization," J. M. Clark, Ch. In *Financing Defense: Federal Tax and Expenditure Policies*, ed. by Albert G. Hart and E. Cary Brown. New York: The Twentieth Century Fund, pp. 149–61.

"Recommendations of the Committee on Economic Stabilization," J. M. Clark, Ch. In *Defense Without Inflation*, by Albert G. Hart. New York: The Twentieth Century Fund, pp. 165–86.

1952 "J. M. Clark on J. B. Clark." In *The Development of Economic Thought*, Henry William Spiegel, ed. New York: John Wiley & Sons, pp. 593–612.

1953 †"Aims of Economic Life as Seen by Economists." In *Goals of Economic Life*, ed. by A. Dudley Ward. New York: Harper and Brothers, pp. 23–51.

"Recommendations of the Committee on Economic Stabilization." J. M. Clark, Ch. In *Defense and the Dollar: Federal Credit and Monetary Policies*, ed. by Albert G. Hart. New York: The Twentieth Century Fund, pp. 189–97.

1954 †"The Interpenetration of Politics and Economics." In *Freedom and Control in Modern Society*, ed. by M. Berger et al. New York: D. Van Nostrand Co., pp. 192–205.

1955 "Competition: Static Models and Dynamic Aspects." *American Economic Review* /s, 45(May):450–62.

†"Economic Welfare in a Free Society." In *National Policy for Economic Welfare at Home and Abroad*, ed. by Robert Lekachman. New York: Doubleday and Co.

†*The Ethical Basis of Economic Freedom* (The Kazanjian Lectures). Westport, Conn.: The Calvin K. Kazanjian Economic Foundation, pp. 46.

1958 "The Uses of Diversity: Competitive Bearings of Diversities in Cost and Demand Functions." *American Economic Review* /s, 48(May):474–82.

WRITINGS ABOUT J. M. CLARK

Notable reviews of Clark's books (in alphabetical order):

Boulding, K. E. 1957. Review of *Economic Institutions and Human Welfare*. In *American Economic Review*, 47(December 1957):1004–5.

Copeland, Morris A. 1925. Review of *Studies in the Economics of Overhead Costs*. In *Political Science Quarterly*, 40(June):296–99.

Dewey, Donald 1963. Review of *Competition as a Dynamic Process*. In *Journal of Political Economy*, 71(February):87–89.

Galbraith, J. K. 1957. Review of *Economic Institutions and Human Welfare*. In *New York Times Book Review*, May 12, p. 3.

Hobson, J. A. 1937. Review of *Preface to Social Economics*. In *Economica*, 4(February):91–93.

Lynd, Robert S. 1948. Review of *Alternative to Serfdom*. In *Saturday Review of Literature*, 31(June 12):24–25.

Peacock, Alan T. 1950. Review of *Alternative to Serfdom*. In *Economica*, 17(February):117–19.

Slichter, Sumner H. 1937. Review of *Planning Public Works*. In *American Economic Review*, 27(March):186–90.

Wright, David McCord 1949. Review of *Alternative to Serfdom*. In *The Journal of Business*, 22(January):67–68.

Selected general appraisals (in alphabetical order)

Dorfman, Joseph 1959. "John Maurice Clark: The Constructive Synthesis of Tradition and the New Dynamics." In *The Economic Mind in American Civilization*. by Dorfman. 5 vols. New York: The Viking Press, 5:438–63. Reprinted in 1966–1969 by Augustus M. Kelley, Publishers, New York.

Gruchy, Allan G. 1947. "The Social Economics of John M. Clark." In *Modern Economic Thought: The American Contribution*, by Gruchy. New York: Prentice-Hall, Inc., pp. 337–402.

Markham, Jesse W. 1968. "Clark, John Maurice." In *International Encyclopedia of the Social Sciences*, ed. by David L. Sills. 17 vols. New York: The Macmillan Co. and the Free Press, 2:508–11.

Marshall, Howard D. 1967. "John Maurice Clark (1884–1963)." In *The Great Economists*. New York: Pitman, pp. 353–59.

McDonald, John 1950. "The Economists." *Fortune*, 42(December): 108–113 et. seq.

Oser, Jacob 1970. "Clark." In *The Evolution of Economic Thought*, 2nd ed., New York: Harcourt, Brace and World, pp. 382–86.

Powers, Edward 1969. *The Social Economics of John Maurice Clark*. Ph.D. diss. Boston College, 1967. Ann Arbor: University Microfilms, Inc., pp. 402.

Seligman, Ben B. 1962. "John Maurice Clark: Social Control in Moderation." In *Main Currents in Modern Economics: Economic Thought Since 1870*, New York: The Free Press, pp. 200–221.

Sievers, Allen M. 1962. "Clark and His Work; Clark the Economic

Philosopher." In *Revolution, Evolution, and the Economic Order,* by Sievers. Englewood Cliffs, N. J.: Prentice-Hall, pp. 127–55.

Suranyi-Unger, T. 1931. *Economics in the Twentieth Century.* ed. by Edwin A. Seligman, translated from the German by Noel D. Moulton. New York: W. W. Norton & Co., Inc., pp. 327–28.

Columbia Essays
on the Great Economists Series
DONALD DEWEY, *GENERAL EDITOR*

J. M. CLARK   *C. ADDISON HICKMAN* $1.95

The sheer volume of John M. Clark's work in economics is matched by its wide-ranging character encompassing at least a dozen fields of economics and by the consistently demanding professional level at which he wrote. In this study of the distinguished American economist and longtime Columbia University professor, C. Addison Hickman presents a lucid, clearly written analysis and evaluation of Clark's major contributions to modern economic theory.

Professor Hickman focuses particularly on Clark's important work in four primary fields of economics. These include:

microeconomics (largely overhead costs and workable competition);

macroeconomics (mostly his "strategic factors" approach to the business cycle, the acceleration principle, and his policy prescriptions for stabilization and full employment);

the economics of welfare (stressing social control, the meaning of welfare, and voluntary pluralism);

and an examination of the discipline of economics (especially its scope, methods, and premises).

In Professor Hickman's view, Clark's ideas on welfare and social control and on constructive approaches to economics as a field of inquiry have been neglected in favor of his other work yet may have at least as much import. This essay fills the gap by giving due attention to Clark's contributions in familiar areas such as overhead costs, workable competition, and the acceleration principle, while providing much-needed compensatory highlighting to his pioneering and prophetic work in welfare and his "sane and healing advice to his economist colleagues concerning their discipline."

In a concluding section, Professor Hickman assesses Clark's durability and his place in the history of thought. Clark is shown to possess diverse skills, a wide-ranging knowledge, a determination to relate theory to reality, and an eminent balance and reasonableness that underscore all of his contributions and defy easy classification in any one "school" or mode of economic thought.

A special feature of this essay is a "Postscript" containing excerpts from the scores of book reviews, biographical sketches and memorial essays written by Clark on the work of his distinguished peers. Included are pieces on such luminaries as Veblen, Keynes, Hayek, Mitchell, Hobson, and Cooley, as well as a piece on his noted economist father, John Bates Clark.

C. Addison Hickman is Vandeveer Professor of Economics at Southern Illinois University.

Columbia University Press
New York and London

ISBN 0-231-03918-2   Printed in U.S.A.